D0071718

How
LATVIA
Came through
the Financial
Crisis

Contents

Tables

Figures

Box

Preface

The world has just gone through the greatest financial crisis since the Great Depression. One of the countries that suffered the most was Latvia, where GDP contracted by 25 percent and unemployment rose to more than 20 percent.

Senior Fellow Anders Åslund has studied the financial crisis in Eastern Europe, and in the spring of 2009 Latvia's Prime Minister Valdis Dombrovskis contacted Åslund and suggested that they write a book about how Latvia came out of the crisis. Åslund is one of the very few international economists who had publicly taken the same position as the Latvian government. Moreover, Dombrovskis thought the Latvian crisis resolution so remarkable that it was worth a serious study in English for an international audience. I agreed that the Peterson Institute should produce such a book.

Latvia offers an interesting case study of the global financial crisis. By 2007, the Latvian economy was seriously overheated, and the extraordinary boom turned into a bust because of a drastic contraction of credit, which become a near complete liquidity squeeze in the fall of 2008. While the prelude to the crisis was a standard boom-bust cycle, the crisis resolution was unusual and more interesting. The conventional wisdom among international economists was that Latvia had no choice but to devalue, but the Latvian government refused. Instead, a broad Latvian consensus opted for what they called an "internal devaluation," which meant severe cuts in wages and public expenditures.

Altogether, Latvia has carried out a fiscal adjustment of 15 percent of GDP, most of which was done through cuts in public expenditures in one single year, 2009. Contrary to many warnings, social peace prevailed. Evidently, devaluation was not needed, and the authors argue that it would not have been beneficial. Latvia has become the pioneer of internal devaluation, which several crisis countries in the eurozone now have to carry out because they have no option of traditional devaluation.

The Latvian stabilization program also represented a new form of international cooperation. Uncharacteristically, the International Monetary Fund provided less than one-quarter of the financing, while both the European Union and friendly neighbors offered the rest. The total funding amounted to more than one-third of Latvia's GDP, rendering it one of the first mega rescue packages. Neither the international cooperation nor the volume of financial support was without controversy.

The Latvian crisis resolution has proven successful. After two years of severe crisis, economic growth has returned. The chronic current account deficit turned into a large surplus in 2009, and the high inflation into minor deflation in 2010. The banking crisis cost much less than anticipated, which is the main reason why Latvia has not needed to use more than half of the international financial support that was offered. In addition to positive economic news, the Dombrovskis government was reelected in parliamentary elections in October 2010, showing that a government can be rewarded for crisis resolution.

The Peter G. Peterson Institute for International Economics is a private, nonprofit institution for the study and discussion of international economic policy. Its purpose is to analyze important issues in that area and to develop and communicate practical new approaches for dealing with them. The Institute is completely nonpartisan.

The Institute is funded by a highly diversified group of philanthropic foundations, private corporations, and interested individuals. About 35 percent of the Institute's resources in our latest fiscal year was provided by contributors outside the United States. The Victor Pinchuk Foundation and the Open Society Institute provided support for this study.

The Institute's Board of Directors bears overall responsibilities for the Institute and gives general guidance and approval to its research program, including the identification of topics that are likely to become important over the medium run (one to three years) and that should be addressed by the Institute. The director, working closely with the staff and outside Advisory Committee, is responsible for the development of particular projects and makes the final decision to publish an individual study.

The Institute hopes that its studies and other activities will contribute to building a stronger foundation for international economic policy around the world. We invite readers of these publications to let us know how they think we can best accomplish this objective.

C. Fred Bergsten
Director
March 2011

Authors' Note

This book is not a memoir, although one of us (Valdis Dombrovskis) has been prime minister of Latvia since March 2009 and had been deeply involved with the country's response to the financial and economic crisis of 2008–10. Instead, it is an economic analysis of the crisis, which hit Latvia particularly hard. Interspersed with the analysis are chronological accounts of how the crisis and its resolution evolved, which we think are helpful in explaining why certain decisions were made. Both of us have been engaged in the Latvian crisis and independently taken very similar policy stands, so we thought it would be useful to write a book together to explain the Latvian policy debate, the actual policy, and the outcomes. We have a strong and shared point of view but also try to present the opposing arguments.

We express all shared opinions, observations, and views in first person plural, but the narrative shifts to first person singular when one of us (Dombrovskis) narrates first-hand accounts of the actual decision-making in the Latvian government and the policy debates and political events surrounding the financial crisis in chapters 5 and 6.

We have benefited from the views and knowledge of many people. We would particularly like to mention Einars Repše, Ilmārs Rimšēvičs, Andris Vilks, and Mats Staffansson. Other important commentators were Bas Bakker, Christoph Rosenberg, Mark Griffiths, Jens Henriksson, Anna-Lisa Trulson Evidon, and Åke Törnqvist. Nazar Kholod did outstanding work as the main research assistant, and Gints Freimanis provided valuable comments. Madona Devasahayam, Susann Luetjen, and Edward A. Tureen of the Peterson Institute publications department skillfully saw the manuscript through the production process.

ANDERS ÅSLUND &
VALDIS DOMBROVSKIS

About the Authors

Anders Åslund is a leading specialist on postcommunist economic transformation with more than 30 years of experience in the field. He is the author of 11 books and the editor of 16. Among his recent books are *How Ukraine Became a Market Economy and Democracy* (2009), *Russia's Capitalist Revolution* (2007), and *How Capitalism Was Built* (2007). He has also published widely, including in *Foreign Affairs*, *Foreign Policy*, *National Interest*, *New York Times*, *Washington Post*, *Financial Times*, and *Wall Street Journal*.

Åslund joined the Peterson Institute for International Economics as senior fellow in 2006. He has worked as an economic adviser to the Russian government (1991–94), to the Ukrainian government (1994–97), and to the president of the Kyrgyz Republic. Before joining the Peterson Institute he was the director of the Russian and Eurasian Program at the Carnegie Endowment for International Peace, and he codirected the Carnegie Moscow Center's project on Post-Soviet Economies.

Previously, he served as a Swedish diplomat in Kuwait, Geneva, Poland, Moscow, and Stockholm. From 1989 until 1994, he was professor and founding director of the Stockholm Institute of Transition Economics at the Stockholm School of Economics. He earned his doctorate from the University of Oxford.

Valdis Dombrovskis has been the Prime Minister of the Republic of Latvia since March 2009. He was also Minister for Regional Development and Local Governments (November–December 2010) and Minister for Children, Family, and Integration Affairs (March–July 2009). From July 2004 to March 2009, he was member of the European Parliament and head of the Latvian delegation in the ETP-ED group. As member of the European Parliament, he was member of the Committee on Budgets and substitute member of Committee on Budgetary Control and Committee on Economic and Monetary matters. He was elected to the Latvian parliament in 2002 and 2010.

From November 2002 to March 2004, Dombrovskis served as Latvia's Minister for Finance. He was founding member of the political party New Era in February 2002. He worked at the Bank of Latvia as macroeconomic specialist (1998-99), senior economist (1999-2001) and chief economist (2001-02).

Dombrovskis has earned degrees in economics and physics from the University of Latvia and Riga Technical University. He has also studied at Mainz University (Germany), and the University of Maryland (United States). He is the author of many publications on economics and politics in various periodicals, journals, and electronic media.

Latvia

NORWAY

Oslo ✪

SWEDEN

Stockholm ✪

Helsinki ✪
Gulf of Finland

Tallinn ✪

ESTONIA

RUSSIAN FEDERATION

Moscow ✪

Gulf of
Riga

Riga ✪

LATVIA

B A L T I C   S E A

LITHUANIA

Vilnius ✪

BELARUS

Minsk ✪

RUSSIAN
FEDERATION

Copenhagen ✪

Berlin ✪

POLAND

Introduction

One of the most remarkable financial crises of 2008–10 has been the one that unfolded in Latvia. The country was already the most overheated economy in the European Union when the crisis hit. Then it suffered a near complete liquidity squeeze, which shaved off no less than one-quarter of its GDP.

Contrary to popular expectation at the time, Latvia did not crumble and social calm prevailed. Its democratic, parliamentary system of government proved perfectly able to handle and resolve the crisis. After two years of output contraction, Latvia's economy began to expand again in 2010 on the back of strong export growth.

The economic policy that helped Latvia recover from the crisis is striking. A broad majority opposed devaluation of the Latvian currency, the lat, and the country has maintained its fixed exchange rate to the euro. Instead Latvia carried out an "internal devaluation" with large cuts in wages and public expenditures as well as strategic reforms in public services. The country benefited from one of the largest international financing packages and became an experiment of cooperation between the International Monetary Fund (IMF) and the European Union.

Motivation

Why write a book about a brief financial crisis in a small country such as Latvia with a population of only 2.2 million? There are many reasons why this topic is worth a book.

Measured as decline in GDP from peak to nadir—25 percent—Latvia experienced the most severe financial crisis in the world during the crisis years of 2008–10. Unemployment, as measured by labor force surveys, peaked in the first quarter of 2010 at 20.7 percent of the active labor force—the worst in the European Union. Yet, in spite of the severity of the crisis, the Latvian economy recovered reasonably quickly and soundly after nine quarters of declining GDP in annualized terms. Latvia stands out as an example of how such a financial crisis can be resolved.

The financial crisis in Latvia, as well as in its Baltic neighbors Estonia and Lithuania, provoked a charged international policy debate. Numerous international economists argued that devaluation was not only necessary but also inevitable. By the end of 2009, however, it became clear that they were wrong.

Instead, all three Baltic countries have pursued "internal devaluations"—cutting public expenditures, wages, and other costs, while carrying out profound structural reforms. When a country needs to address underlying structural inefficiencies in the economy, internal devaluation is preferable to exchange rate devaluation, which offers only temporary relief from cost pressures while avoiding long overdue reforms.

An intriguing aspect of the crisis has been the political economy of Latvia's financial stabilization, which was carried out by a coalition government of some four parties, sometimes with a minority in the parliament, with one government collapsing in the middle of the crisis. Even so, the Latvian government succeeded in overcoming the crisis, and the Latvian people offered strong support to the government's policy. Social unrest was minimal, and extremism nearly absent. Most remarkably, the incumbent government that shepherded the nation through the hardship won the parliamentary elections in October 2010, while traditional populism lost out and ethnic tensions were reduced.

The Latvian stabilization program was accompanied by a large international financing package of €7.5 billion ($10.5 billion), 37 percent of Latvia's GDP. Soon, several larger packages were formed for other countries in crisis, but Latvia's was the pioneer. The country has used only 58 percent of the financing available and is already out of the crisis with a reasonable public debt of 42 percent of GDP at the end of 2010, suggesting that the large-scale rescue package was successful.

The international support package for Latvia was composed in a new way. The IMF contributed less than one-quarter of the total, while the European Union offered more than one-third and European neighbors most of the balance, creating a new form of cooperation between the IMF and the European Commission.

Because of the severity of the crisis, the Latvian government had no choice but to undertake large and swift reductions in public expenditures. The total fiscal adjustment has been estimated at 11 percent of GDP in 2009 alone, and most of it involved cuts in public outlays. These large cuts made long-delayed structural reforms in the public sector necessary, notably in public administration, health care, and education. These reforms are likely to generate positive supply effects that will contribute to greater growth in the future.

Key Lessons

Latvia has done what many said could not be done. We emphasize nine lessons on the economics of financial crisis and its political economy.

A key lesson from Latvia's financial crisis resolution is that devaluation is neither a panacea nor a necessity that many economists make it out to be. Latvia suffered from financial overheating. The country's competitiveness needed to improve, which was better done by reducing the bloated salaries and costs. The cure to overheating was to stop excessive short-term capital inflows, which did not require devaluation. The financial crisis erupted because of a sudden stop of international liquidity, and Latvia had to quickly mobilize more liquidity to deal with the crisis. In addition, the steady exchange rate parity forced Latvia to undertake long-overdue structural reforms. The alleged risk of a vicious, deflationary cycle was never real. For a small and open economy such as Latvia, prices are largely determined by the surrounding markets. As the pass through of inflation would have been great, devaluation would not have been effective in restoring competitiveness.

Second, the Latvian people were motivated by their desire for full European integration with early adoption of the euro, which led them to focus on two nominal anchors: a fixed exchange rate and a budget deficit below 3 percent of GDP, so that Latvia could accede to the Economic and Monetary Union as early as possible.

Third, Latvia's experience with fiscal adjustment shows the advantages of carrying out as much of the adjustment as possible early on. Hardship is best concentrated to a short period, when people are ready for sacrifice.

Fourth, more than three-quarters of the fiscal adjustment came from cuts in public expenditures, suggesting that they are economically and politically better than tax hikes. The most popular budget adjustments were cuts of salaries and benefits of senior civil servants and state enterprise managers as well as the reduction in public service positions. Latvians have remained strongly committed to their flat income taxes.

Fifth, the large and frontloaded international rescue effort was appropriate and has been successful. Today, it is difficult to understand that the size of the Latvian package could be controversial. Much larger emergency credits in relation to GDP than before were needed because of greater globalization, and the Latvian crisis was primarily caused by the dearth of international liquidity. It was not a solidity crisis.

Sixth, a strange myth has evolved that affluent democracies are politically unable to undertake large cuts in public expenditures. Latvia, as well as its Baltic neighbors, showed that these vibrant democracies were perfectly capable of reducing their public expenditures by about one-tenth of GDP in one year.

Seventh, the benefits of stable government have been greatly exaggerated. It is more important that a government be adequate than stable, and a precrisis government is rarely a suitable anticrisis government. Latvia benefited from being able to switch government quickly during the crisis. This was possible because of unstable coalition governments, which arise from a parliamentary system with proportional elections. Thus, parliamentary systems with many parties, leading to coalition governments and frequent government changes, may be beneficial for the resolution of macroeconomic crises.

Eighth, the bottom line is that populism is not very popular in a serious crisis when the population understands the severity of the crisis and wants a sensible and resolute government that can handle the crisis as forcefully as is necessary. Thus, the Latvian anticrisis government was able to win the parliamentary elections on October 2, 2010. The big losers in the 2010 elections were oligarchs who tried to exploit populism.

Finally, the international macroeconomic discussion was not useful but even harmful. Whenever a crisis erupts anywhere in the world, a choir of famous international economists proclaim that it is "exactly" like some other recent crisis—the worse the crisis, the more popular the parallel. Soon, prominent economists led by *New York Times* columnist Paul Krugman claimed that "Latvia is the new Argentina." A fundamental problem is their reliance on a brief list of "stylized facts," never bothering to find out the facts.

Structure of the Book

The structure of this book is chronological-thematic. Chapter 1 offers a brief background on Latvia's history and postcommunist transition to market economics and democracy. Chapter 2 discusses the boom of 2004–07 and the causes of the ensuing financial crisis. Chapter 3 presents the policies the government had to choose from in the fourth quarter of 2008 after the crisis had erupted, the initial government program, as well as the international assistance package. Chapter 4 focuses on the key intellectual debate and the biggest choice that the country faced: to devalue or not. Chapter 5 recounts the crisis resolution and the economic and political drama in 2009. Chapter 6 describes the early signs of recovery in 2010, when the financial crisis finally abated. Chapter 7 presents our conclusions, an important one of which is that Latvia is committed to adopting the euro as soon as possible, a goal that the government kept in mind when formulating its crisis resolution strategy.

In most regards, developments in the three Baltic countries took place in parallel during the financial crisis. However, we focus solely on Latvia as a case study of the global financial crisis of 2008–10 and largely avoid too many references to Estonia and Lithuania.

We have used a large volume of official government material in Latvian as sources and for readers' convenience have translated as accurately as possible all quotes and document titles into English. News reports we cite from two Latvian news agencies, LETA and DELFI, have also been suitably translated.

1

Latvia's Post-Soviet Transition

The collapse of the Soviet Union, beginning in the late 1980s, was a dream come true for the Latvian people, who had never voluntarily joined that state. Their great dream—to restore national sovereignty and independence to their country—was fulfilled in August 1991. The next daunting task was to establish a normal, functioning market economy to escape the post-Soviet economic chaos. It needed to be combined with the building of a normal parliamentary democracy as in Western Europe.[1]

A Bitter Struggle for Independence

Latvia has had a difficult history, particularly in the last century. Shortly after the end of World War I, in November 1918, the Latvian government declared Latvia an independent state for the first time in history. But within weeks, communists supported by Soviet Russia took control. After brief communist rule and independence battles against both German and Russian troops, Latvia signed the Latvian-Soviet Peace Treaty on August 11, 1920, and Soviet Russia recognized Latvia as an independent and sovereign state. Twenty years of independence followed.

Few countries suffered as much as Latvia during World War II. On August 23, 1939, the Soviet Union and Nazi Germany concluded the Molotov-Ribbentrop Non-Aggression Pact, which divided a number of countries between the two states. The pact awarded the three Baltic states to the Soviet Union, thus sealing Latvia's fate. On the basis of the Molotov-Ribbentrop Pact, Soviet troops invaded and occupied Latvia in June 1940. The Soviets deported some 35,000 Latvians, mainly members of the Latvian intellectual, political, and business elite, to Siberia, where most of them perished. Nazi Germany then invaded in June 1941, killing some 70,000 Jews in the Holocaust and some 18,000 Latvians during the occupation. In 1944, the Red Army came back and occupied Latvia, incorporating it into the Soviet Union as one of its 15 union republics. The Soviets deported or executed over 100,000 Latvians, while at least 150,000 fled to the West.[2] Latvia was one of the most divided countries, with one part fighting in the Latvian legion against the communists and another conscripted into the Soviet army—father and son could have been on different sides of the front line.

After World War II, Latvia's politics and economy were completely soviet-ized, and the nation became subject to intense russification. Latvia's significant Russian-speaking population expanded rapidly, as Russians, Ukrainians, and Belarusians moved to the comparatively well developed Latvia, while Latvian birth rates were low. According to the Soviet census of 1989, ethnic Latvians made up only 52 percent of the population, and many Latvians feared they would become a minority in their own homeland. Most of the population in Riga spoke Russian as their native tongue. The Latvian nation struggled for its survival.

The Latvians—like the Estonians and the Lithuanians—were never recon-ciled to their incorporation into the Soviet Union, longing for its demise and for national independence. Historically and geographically, they related to the Scandinavian countries and saw no reason for their occupation by the Soviets. The Balts got their chance with political liberalization under Soviet leader Mikhail Gorbachev in the late 1980s. While Gorbachev considered the Balts the most liberal and enlightened people in the Soviet Union, he did not under-stand that their goal was not only political and economic liberalization but also national independence.

As soon as Soviet repression began to ease, the Estonians, Latvians, and Lithuanians all started working for their national independence. Their first steps toward independence were disguised as environmental protests, because such causes were permitted by the Soviet power structures. Soon, however, national attention turned to the key issue, condemnation of the Molotov-Ribbentrop Pact and the ensuing Soviet occupation of the Baltics. Developments in the three Baltic countries were largely parallel. Estonia and Lithuania competed for the lead, while Latvia followed suit, held back some-what since it harbored the largest Soviet military forces.

In each of the three countries, a broad popular front was established in 1988 to restore independence. They were primarily nationalist but also demo-cratic and liberal. The Lithuanian and Estonian Communist Parties tried to keep up with the nationalists, liberalizing their policies and practices, as did the communists in Poland and Hungary, while the Latvian Communist Party split in the middle, with one faction being truly hardline. In the republican elections in February–March 1990, the Baltic popular fronts won more than two-thirds majorities in all three parliaments and assumed executive power in all three republics in the spring of 1990, though Soviet power still controlled them from Moscow. The Baltic states declared independence from the Soviet Union, which refused to accept it.

Latvia differed from Estonia and Lithuania in several regards. The country harbored larger and more important Soviet military installations than its neighbors. Riga has been the dominant city in the region for centuries, having attracted a large Russian population even before World War II. With its large and good ports, Latvia was the main transit country in the Baltics. Riga's large industrial enterprises, producing phones and microbuses, overshadowed those in the neighboring countries. Because of its greater strategic significance, Latvia was more tightly controlled by Moscow than its neighbors.

The abortive hardline August 1991 coup in Moscow brought real independence to the Baltic states. Immediately afterward, Russian President Boris Yeltsin recognized their independence. On September 6, the Soviet Union did so as well, and then all other countries followed suit. On September 17, the United Nations welcomed the three Baltic states as members, having ascertained their independence and sovereignty. On August 31, 1994, after lengthy negotiations, the last Russian troops left Latvian territory.

These three nations and their civil societies matured in a comparatively lengthy process of democratization. They were ripe for full democracy with multiparty elections and radical market economic reform. Their national objectives were firmly set: to turn their backs on Russia, to reintegrate with the West, and to establish Western political, economic, and legal systems. As in Central and Southeastern Europe, the slogans were: "We want a normal society" and a "return to Europe." A normal society was understood as West European democracy with a market economy, private property rights, and the rule of law. A return to Europe meant their integration into West European economic and political organizations, notably membership in the European Union but also in the Council of Europe and the North Atlantic Treaty Organization (NATO).

Radical Transition to a Normal Market Economy

In 1991, when Latvia left the Soviet Union, the Soviet economy was collapsing in every sense: GDP was approaching free fall; the Soviet budget deficit was about 31 percent of GDP; prices were skyrocketing, but even so shortages prevailed as prices were still state controlled; and no foreign currency reserves were on hand, which disrupted most trade. The total official fall in Latvia's GDP from 1990 to 1993 was no less than 49 percent.[3] Although official statistics exaggerate the decline for various technical reasons, the slump was horrendous.

Establishing a functioning economy was vital for the newly reborn nation. Its reform package contained standard elements of systemic change: liberalization of prices and trade, macroeconomic stabilization, and privatization. All kinds of national institutions and legislation had to be established, often from scratch.[4]

The most critical task after independence was achieving monetary stability. The Baltic nationalists were determined to leave the monetary mess of the ruble zone behind by exiting as soon as possible and establishing their own national currencies, which they saw as the best border against Russia. They disregarded transition costs, because they saw a West-oriented, stable market economy as the best long-term option. The International Monetary Fund (IMF), which Latvia joined in May 1992, was the main international agency involved, but it considered the ruble zone a political issue and preferred to be neutral. Yet it assisted the Baltic states with the launch of their own currencies in mid-1992.[5]

As so often happened in the Baltic transition, Estonia took the lead and went for a truly radical reform, focusing on its currency and exchange rate policy. In June 1992, it broke out of the ruble zone and established its independent currency in order to distance itself from the Soviet Union and to facilitate financial stabilization. Estonia adopted a currency board, which had several specific properties. First, the exchange rate was permanently fixed, first to the deutsche mark and later to the euro. Second, international reserves covered the whole money supply. Third, the current account balance determined the money supply, which meant not only that domestic authorities could not pursue monetary policy, and interest rates were set by the market, but also that capital inflow would cause inflation. Fourth, the Estonians willingly committed themselves to balance the state budget, disavowing public borrowing and thus government bonds.[6]

This full-fledged currency board was a robust arrangement, creating credibility both at home and abroad, and the balance of payments would determine inflation. While the IMF did not initiate the currency board, it accepted the idea. Currency boards were considered appropriate for small, open economies that had been subject to high inflation, which suited the Baltic states.[7] Estonia introduced the currency board and stabilization policy with a bang in June 1992, combined with an IMF standby program and substantial Western financial support. Since a low exchange rate was chosen, it was easily defended, but the drawback was sizable real appreciation, which kept inflation rather high. The currency board, together with completely free trade, minimized government interference in foreign trade. A concern, however, was the absence of a lender of last resort.

Estonia and Latvia pursued similar free-market radicalism in their macroeconomic policy. Latvia broke out of the ruble zone and launched its currency in July 1992. It undertook an equally impressive stabilization, with an IMF program and large international financial support, but the heart of its stabilization was strict monetary policy, spearheaded by Einars Repše, who was Latvia's predominant reformer and led Latvian macroeconomic policy for a decade as the chairman of the Bank of Latvia from 1991 to 2001. Latvia was determined to succeed as an independent state regardless of cost. Although it largely followed Estonia, it did not adopt a full-fledged currency board. One reason was that Latvia did not have such large international reserves. Officially, Latvia initially pursued a managed float, which was really an informal peg,

Figure 1.1 Inflation, 1991–95

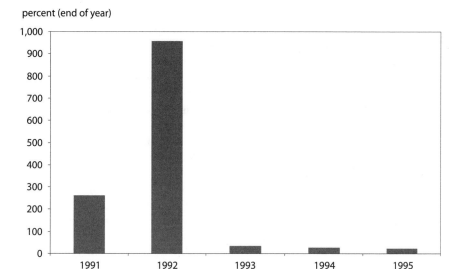

percent (end of year)

Source: European Bank for Reconstruction and Development, *Transition Report 1997*, www.ebrd.org.

and from February 1994 it pegged to special drawing rights but in practice pursued a quasi currency board. Its inflation plummeted from 959 percent in 1992 to 35 percent in 1993 (figure 1.1), but only in 1997 did it reach the single digits—7 percent, after which inflation hovered around 3 percent a year.

In the early 1990s, Latvia quickly adopted all the many laws required for the construction of a democratic society based on the rule of law. It returned to its Constitution of 1922, which was amended. All the main laws for a normal market economy were revived or adopted anew.

In fiscal policy, Latvia followed Estonia's radical lead. Unlike other post-communist states, the three Baltic states managed to sharply cut harmful public expenditures, such as enterprise and price subsidies, from the outset. Latvia's public expenditures stabilized around a moderate 38 percent of GDP. In 1993–95, it introduced a simple and sound tax system with four broad taxes, which were sufficient to balance its expenditures: a flat personal income tax of 25 percent, a value-added tax of 18 percent, and a flat corporate profit tax of 25 percent, which was successively diminished to 15 percent. The old social payroll tax was replaced with social security contributions, which were gradually reduced from 37 to 33 percent. This tax system was simple and efficient and has not gone through any major change since the mid-1990s.[8]

Privatization was seen as a matter of morals and justice as well as the basis of a market economy. The old property rights of independent Latvia were still remembered and cherished. The fundamental principle of justice was restitution, returning everything to the original owner or legal inheritors, which was widely perceived as legitimate. Restitution of farmland and real estate was carried out quickly and with great success but that of medium-sized and large enterprises was not really possible. Small enterprises were easily sold off, and some mass privatization was carried out, with vouchers distributed to all. Privatization proceeded fast and by 1998, two-thirds of GDP originated in the private sector. However, a few large enterprises that were both economically and politically difficult to privatize lingered in state ownership.[9] While economically largely successful, as in most postcommunist countries, privatization was also viewed as an unjust and corrupt process during which much of the public property ended up in the hands of a selected few at ridiculously low prices.

The weakest part of Latvia's early postcommunist transition was deregulation, which was not quite as radical as in the other Baltic countries. Latvia possesses two of the biggest Baltic ports, Riga and Ventspils, through which considerable transit trade took place. Traders made fortunes in the early transition on arbitrage between free and regulated prices in commodity trade. Such rent-seeking business interests were strong in Latvia and resulted in distortion of the legislative process to the benefit of a few big traders, so-called oligarchs, who also appeared as a result of privatization. They formed strong vested interests that continue to haunt Latvia.[10]

A spectacular achievement of most postcommunist countries was the instant adoption of current account convertibility, which applied to foreign trade and tourist traffic, while capital account convertibility was adopted progressively from 1994, with the Baltic states taking the lead.[11] Estonia was the first postcommunist country to opt for full convertibility in 1994, which greatly facilitated foreign trade liberalization.

Multiple international agreements reinforced trade liberalization.[12] Most important was Latvia's cooperation with the European Union, based on Latvians' determination to become an EU member. Its Trade and Cooperation Agreement with the European Community came into force as early as February 1993, and in June 1994 Latvia signed an EU Free Trade Agreement, which came into force in January 1995. In June 1995, Latvia concluded the "Europe Agreement," an association agreement with the European Union. It aimed at a broad integration of Latvia into the European Union, not only lowering barriers to trade but also establishing a framework for political dialogue and harmonization of legislation. The Europe Agreement provided for free trade in industrial goods within ten years, with the European Union reducing protectionist measures faster than the East-Central European countries.[13] On October 13, 1995, Latvia formally applied for EU membership, and on October 13, 1999, the European Commission recommended that member states open negotiations with Latvia. By 2000, 65 percent of Latvia's exports went to the then 15 EU members. At that time, 81 percent of its exports was directed to the current 27 EU members. This share moderated to 72 percent by 2009, since traditional trade with Russia somewhat recovered. Estonia and Lithuania are now among Latvia's foremost trading partners.

As the EU accession process started, Latvia gradually adopted the whole common body of EU law, *acquis communautaire*, currently amounting to some 125,000 pages. Especially during the years 1999–2003, Latvia implemented a far-reaching reform process, adjusting multiple laws, rules, standards, and regulations to EU norms. Consequently, Latvia's economy became much more efficient and productive. This major transformation is often understated because it consisted of thousands of details rather than major legal codes.

To Latvia, accession to the European Union was central, and its earlier application for membership in the World Trade Organization (WTO) was only a sideshow. It took until February 10, 1999, for Latvia to become a member of the WTO; by then its assumption of EU standards was already well under way.

In the first half of 1995, soon after its vigorous stabilization attempt, Latvia faced a major banking crisis. Banks had been caught off-guard by the sudden macroeconomic stabilization, and Baltija Bank, Latvia's biggest bank, turned out to be insolvent. It had been betting against the lat, attracting lat deposits offering interest rates of up to 90 percent a year. It had pursued reckless expansion and thought it could overrule the Bank of Latvia. After some hesitation, the Bank of Latvia went for a radical solution. Revealing extensive fraud, it closed and bankrupted 15 commercial banks, accounting for 35 to 40 percent of the banking assets and 53 percent of household deposits. The shareholders lost everything, and the depositors received only partial compensation, since they had taken obvious risks, betting on high interest rates. Banks were forced to accept truly hard budget constraints.[14] The banking crisis impeded Latvia's economic growth, which had just about turned positive in 1994, and in 1995 its GDP contracted by 2.1 percent, but the harsh resolution cleansed the Latvian banking system.

The Latvian economy was finally taking off, with a GDP growth of 8.3 percent in 1997, when the Russian financial crisis hit in 1998. Latvia escaped with limited damage as it was no longer very dependent on the Russian market, and the growth rate fell only to 3.3 percent in 1999. Latvian enterprises responded with energetic restructuring, initiating a decade of magnificent growth (figure 1.2). Latvia had caught up with the reform leaders in the Baltics and Central Europe and seemed unstoppable.[15]

From 2000, the Latvian market economy was in excellent shape: Inflation was low, government finances close to balance, and a period of extraordinary economic growth started. The nation that had suffered so much in the 20th century appeared to have struck gold in the early 21st century.

A paper from the European Commission characterizes the Baltic transition in rosy but fair terms:

> The reform process was highly successful in reducing the role of the state and reorienting the Baltic economies towards a market system, and thus helping these countries meet the Copenhagen criteria and become eligible for EU accession. Overall, institutional convergence was more rapid in the Baltic countries...than on average in other New Member States, as shown by standard indicators of governance and institutional quality.[16]

Figure 1.2   Annual GDP growth, 1991–2012e

percent

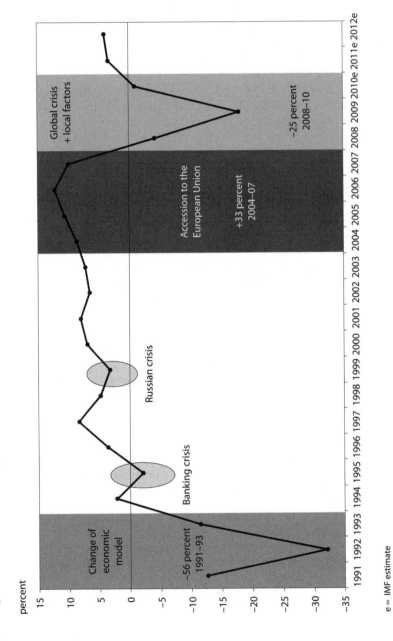

e = IMF estimate

Source: IMF, *World Economic Outlook* database, October 2010 (accessed on November 23, 2010).

Evolution of Latvia's Democratic Politics

Ever since Latvia became independent, freedom and democracy have prevailed.[17] It has a parliamentary system, with a president with limited powers elected by the parliament. The country held parliamentary elections in 1993, 1995, and then regularly every four years since 1998.

Two dividing lines have characterized Latvian politics since 1991, ethnicity and reform versus vested interests. Since independence, ethnic Latvians have dominated all the ruling parties. Nation building was naturally the main goal of the early post-Soviet period, which involved clarifying the right to Latvian citizenship and the official standing of the Latvian language. Ethnic Russians (and Ukrainians and Belarusians) have tended to gather in a couple of parties. To date, none of them has entered any government, because they have refused to accept the basic principles of Latvia's statehood and foreign policy.

The center right has dominated Latvian politics, so ideology has not been a dividing line. On September 10, 1991, the parliament banned the Latvian Communist Party as hostile to Latvia's independence. In 1994, the Socialist Party of Latvia was founded to succeed the Communist Party, but it never gained much popularity, which is also true of social democrats.

Latvia has many political parties, and they are built around personalities rather than ideologies as their political views have been so similar. They have tended to merge into blocs. Usually, six to seven blocs or parties have been represented in parliament, which has meant that three to four parties have been necessary to form a coalition government. As a result of intense jockeying between the parties, each government has lasted for little more than one year on average, but that has not hindered the reform process, since the political views have been so similar. If anything, government instability has promoted reform, because corruption scandals tended to bring down governments.

The other dividing line has been between reform and the vested interests of big businessmen known as oligarchs. Initially, reformers and big businessmen cohabited in the same center-right parties, because the interests of reformers and business coincided to a great extent. Over time, their interests have grown apart, and reformers and businessmen have increasingly separated into different parties.

Corruption, or more politely stated commercial abuse of power, has been a key concern, with some big businessmen having been accused of malfeasance. It has dominated the political debate and brought down the government on several occasions, a healthy sign that the people have not accepted the malfunctioning of the state.[18] A World Bank survey in 1998 showed that the two institutions perceived as most dishonest in Latvia were customs and traffic police, followed by courts, licensing and regulatory agencies, state police, and local municipalities, whereas health care and education involved little corruption.[19] Latvia has carried out a large number of legislative and enforcement measures to reduce corruption, seeking assistance from the World Bank as early as 1996.

Figure 1.3 Corruption Perception Index, 2000–10

index (0 = highly corrupt; 10 = highly clean)

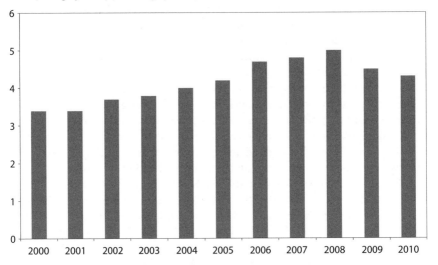

Source: Transparency International, www.transparency.org (accessed on November 30, 2010).

The EU and NATO accession processes provided constant pressure to reinforce anticorruption policy.

While many of Latvia's problems were common to most postcommunist countries, the greatest concern was what the World Bank labels "state capture," the control by a few powerful individuals of key levers of the state for their own benefit.[20] State capture was identified with a few big businessmen, who played a major role in Latvian politics and were suspected of exercising undue influence in major state procurements and privatizations.

To combat corruption, the government set up a Corruption Prevention Council in 1997, and in 2002 it established an independent anticorruption authority, the Corruption Prevention and Combating Bureau (KNAB). It became a hot issue in Latvian politics. Since its establishment, KNAB has been plagued by strife over its powers, its cases, and its appointees, showing that it was a serious effort but that the power of malign forces was substantial.[21]

Overall, because of the great attention devoted to corruption and the free media, Latvia's rating on Transparency International's Corruption Perception Index steadily improved from 2000 until 2008 but declined slightly during the financial crisis (figure 1.3).

By 2004, Latvia appeared to be an astounding success story. In 13 years, it had reestablished itself as an independent and sovereign nation. It had become a full-fledged and well-functioning democracy with a competitive market economy based on predominant private ownership. The rule of law had been secured. Latvia had become a member of both the European Union and NATO. This still poor nation was set for an extraordinary economic expansion. Little did it know that this boom would become far too extraordinary, turning into a bust in the ensuing three years.

Notes

1. Two overall sources for this chapter are Anders Åslund, *Building Capitalism: The Transformation of the Former Soviet Bloc* (New York: Cambridge University Press, 2002); and Anders Åslund, *How Capitalism Was Built: The Transformation of Central and Eastern Europe, Russia, and Central Asia* (New York: Cambridge University Press, 2007).

2. For Latvian history, see Andrejs Plakans, *The Latvians: A Short History* (Stanford: Hoover Institution Press, 1995); Anatol Lieven, *The Baltic Revolution: Estonia, Latvia, Lithuania, and the Path to Independence* (New Haven, CT: Yale University Press, 1993).

3. United Nations Economic Commission for Europe, *Economic Survey of Europe*, no. 1: 225 (New York: United Nations, 2000).

4. The literature on the Baltic market economic transition is substantial and good, notably, Ardo Hansson, "The Trouble with the Rouble: Monetary Reform in the Former Soviet Union," in *Changing the Economic System in Russia*, ed. Anders Åslund and Richard Layard (New York: St. Martin's Press, 1993, 163–82); Seija Lainela and Pekka Sutela, *The Baltic Economies in Transition* (Helsinki: Bank of Finland, 1994); Biswajit Banarjee, Vincent Koen, Thomas Krueger, Mark S. Lutz, Michael Marrese, and Tapio O. Saavalainen, "Road Maps of the Transition: The Baltics, the Czech Republic, Hungary, and Russia," International Monetary Fund Occasional Paper 127 (Washington: International Monetary Fund, 1995); Brian Vanarkadie and Mats Karlsson, eds., *Economic Survey of the Baltic Republics* (New York: New York University Press, 1992).

5. Ardo Hansson, "Macroeconomic Stabilization in the Baltic States," in *Macroeconomic Stabilization in Transition Countries*, ed. Mario I. Blejer and Marko Skreb (New York: Cambridge University Press, 1997, 256–80); Julian Berengaut, Augusto López-Laros, Françoise Le Gall, Dennis Jones, Richard Stern, Ann-Margaret Westin, Effie Psalida, and Pietro Garribaldi, "The Baltic Countries: From Economic Stabilization to EU Accession," International Monetary Fund Occasional Paper no. 173 (Washington: International Monetary Fund, 1998).

6. Steve H. Hanke, Lars Jonung, and Kurt Schuler, *Monetary Reform for a Free Estonia: A Currency Board Solution* (Stockholm: SNS Förlag, 1992); Ardo H. Hansson and Jeffrey D. Sachs, "Crowning the Estonian Kroon," *Transition* 3, no. 9: 1–3 (Washington: World Bank, 1992).

7. John Williamson, *What Role for Currency Boards?* (Washington: Institute for International Economics, 1995).

8. Liam Ebrill, Oleh Havrylyshyn, et al., "Reforms of Tax Policy and Tax Administration in the CIS Countries and the Baltics," International Monetary Fund Occasional Paper 175 (Washington: International Monetary Fund, 1999).

9. Roman Frydman, Andrzej Rapaczynski, John S. Earle, et al., *The Privatization Process in Russia, Ukraine, and the Baltic States* (Budapest: Central European University Press, 1993).

10. The seminal article on rent seeking during postcommunist transition is Joel Hellman, "Winners Take All: The Politics of Partial Reform in Postcommunist Transitions," *World Politics* 50, no. 2 (1998): 203–34.

11. European Bank for Reconstruction and Development, *Transition Report 1997* (London: EBRD, 1997, 88).

12. Michael Leidy and Ali Ibrahim, "Recent Trade Policies and an Approach to Further Reform in the Baltics, Russia, and Other Countries of the Former Soviet Union," International Monetary Fund Working Paper no. 71 (Washington: International Monetary Fund, 1996).

13. Julian Berengaut, Augusto López-Laros, Françoise Le Gall, Dennis Jones, Richard Stern, Ann-Margaret Westin, Effie Psalida, and Pietro Garribaldi, "The Baltic Countries: From Economic Stabilization to EU Accession," International Monetary Fund Occasional Paper 173 (Washington: International Monetary Fund, 1998); European Bank for Reconstruction and Development, *Transition Report 1994* (London: EBRD, 1994).

14. Ardo H. Hansson and Triinu Tombak, "Banking Crises in the Baltic States: Causes, Solutions, and Lessons," in *Financial Sector Transformation: Lessons from Economies in Transition*, ed. Mario I. Blejer and Marko Skreb (New York: Cambridge University Press, 1999, 195–236); Alex Fleming and Samuel Talley, "The Latvian Banking Crisis, April" (Washington: World Bank, 1996); Imants Paeglis, "Troubling Bank Failures in Latvia and Lithuania," *Transition* 2, no. 10 (1996): 14–17.

15. Organization for Economic Cooperation and Development, *OECD Economic Surveys: The Baltic States* (Paris: OECD, 2000).

16. Servaas Deroose, Elena Flores, Gabriele Giudice, and Alessandro Turrini, "The Tale of the Baltics: Experiences, Challenges Ahead and Main Lessons," ECFIN Economic Brief, no. 10 (European Commission, July 2010, 2).

17. For a detailed history of independence, see Anatol Lieven, *The Baltic Revolution: Estonia, Latvia, Lithuania, and the Path to Independence* (New Haven, CT: Yale University Press, 1993). The best study of Latvian foreign policy is Lars Peter Fredén, *Återkomsten: Svensk säkerhetspolitik och de baltiska ländernas första år i självständighet 1991-1994* ["The Return: Swedish Security Policy and the Baltic Countries' First Years of Independence 1991-1994"] (Stockholm: Atlantis, 2006).

18. Ivan Krastev, *Shifting Obsessions: Three Essays on Politics of Anti-Corruption* (Budapest: CEU Press, 2004).

19. James Anderson, "Corruption in Latvia: Survey Evidence" (World Bank Report, photocopy, December 16, 1998, 21).

20. Open Society Institute, "Corruption and Anti-Corruption Policy in Latvia" (mimeo, 2002).

21. Ibid.

2

The Boom, 2004–07

When Latvia joined the European Union and the North Atlantic Treaty Organization (NATO) in 2004, Latvians saw their two great desires fulfilled. They had "rejoined Europe," and the country looked better than ever. The "Baltic tigers," as Latvia, Estonia, and Lithuania came to be called, were rightly perceived as Europe's response to the four East Asian tigers, Hong Kong, Singapore, South Korea, and Taiwan, which for years delivered high economic growth based on fast export growth and high investment ratios.

However, the East Asian tigers had just gone through their financial crisis of 1997–98, and the Baltic states were about to suffer a similar fate, as clouds were gathering in the Baltic sky. As a member of the European Union, Latvia could have no capital controls (not that it desired any), and in order to facilitate early adoption of the euro, Latvia maintained a fixed exchange rate to the euro. Since its business conditions were excellent as well, the country attracted large capital inflows, generating a huge credit expansion, which in turn fueled a spectacular surge in real estate prices, rising inflation, and a substantial current account deficit. This boom based on foreign credit quickly became unsustainable.

Latvia's government during these boom years was quite complacent, presumably because times were very good. Rather than preparing for the inevitable future storm, the government distributed the goodies as they arrived.

EU Accession Crowning the Success of Transition

Latvia joined the European Union on May 1, 2004. Optimism abounded, and economic growth, which had been high since 2000, accelerated. The country enjoyed double-digit growth of an astounding average of 11 percent a year for the three years 2005–07, and in 2006 GDP rose by as much as 12 percent.

Exchange rate policy was a central element of Latvia's economic policy. Fixed exchange rates had served as nominal anchors for macroeconomic stabilization in all three Baltic countries. As a European Commission paper put it: "Credible pegs fostered policy discipline and were among the attractive features for foreign investors."[1] The three Baltic countries wanted to adopt the euro as soon as possible. Their national currencies were already tied to the euro and adopting it was the natural exit from their currency boards. In addition, they were small open economies with much of their trade taking place in euro or pegged to the euro. Estonia and Lithuania joined the European Exchange Rate Mechanism (ERM II) immediately after their EU accession in 2004 and Latvia did so in 2005.

The Baltic countries presumed that they would be able to adopt the euro within three years and opted to maintain their fixed exchange rates with the euro. The European Central Bank (ECB) and the European Commission accepted that, but on the condition that the Balts forgo the standard ECB commitment to supply automatic and unlimited foreign exchange intervention and financing whenever an exchange rate in ERM II reached its fluctuation margins. At the time, nobody thought much about this, since the Baltic economies were Europe's star performers, expecting no need for emergency funding.

An EU country that wants to adopt the euro must belong to the ERM II for two years and fulfill the Maastricht criteria outlined in Article 140 of the Treaty on the Functioning of the European Union, and specified elsewhere, before it is allowed to adopt the euro:

- Price stability: Average inflation rate one year prior to entry must not exceed the average of the lowest three inflation rates of the EU member countries by more than 1.5 percentage points (which usually meant close to 3 percent a year).
- The public sector deficit should not exceed 3 percent of GDP.
- The public debt should not surpass 60 percent of GDP.
- The normal fluctuation margins (+/-2.25 percent) within ERM II should be observed for at least two years. Latvia limited this fluctuation to +/-1 percent.
- The average long-term nominal interest rate must not be higher than the average of the corresponding rates of the three lowest-inflation countries by more than 2 percentage points.[2]

On March 29, 2004, Latvia joined NATO as a full member. It became part of the alliance of the willing and sent troops on the calling of the United States and NATO both to Iraq and Afghanistan. While NATO membership did not have any direct economic consequences, it was another sign to foreign investors that Latvia was a secure area of investment. Latvia had arrived.

Figure 2.1 Annual growth in credit, 2000–10

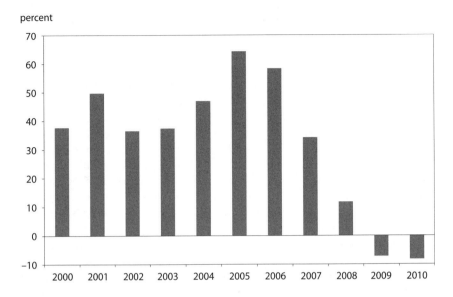

percent

Source: Bank of Latvia, www.bank.lv (accessed on January 24, 2011).

Capital Inflows Overheat the Economy

The surprise was the huge capital inflows the Baltic countries attracted. After all, these countries had just gained independence, established democracy, built capitalism, and escaped from near four-digit inflation. Their success was stunning, but even so the capital inflows were amazing. Before entering the European Union, the Baltic countries had been compelled to relinquish capital controls, which they had been happy to do, but as they maintained a fixed exchange rate, they could not stop the huge, unanticipated capital inflows.

The Russian financial crisis of 1998 had spurred consolidation of the Latvian banking system. Numerous small Latvian banks merged, and primarily Swedish banks started buying them up. By 2007, four banks accounted for three-quarters of Latvia's banking assets. Three were the big Swedish banks Swedbank, SEB, and Nordea, but the second biggest bank was Latvian Parex Bank. In addition, Latvia had more than 30 small local banks. None of the big banks received much local financing through deposits. Instead, they financed themselves cheaply through the European wholesale market, leaving Latvia in a hamster's wheel: When inflation rose, the real interest rate became more negative, boosting credit demand.

By most measures Latvia's extraordinary credit boom outsized most other credit booms with an annual credit expansion of 37 to 64 percent from 2000 to 2006,[3] which peaked in 2005–06 when the amount of credit in the economy more than doubled (figure 2.1). No restrictions impeded lending, and real estate speculation was not taxed.[4] Several forces drove the fast credit expansion. The primary cause was Latvia's attractive business climate and high economic growth. Second, the fixed exchange rate made investment in Latvia seem close to risk-free. Third, credit demand was driven by a sharp decline in the country's real interest rates, which eventually turned negative as inflation rose. Fourth, for the three Swedish banks in Latvia the Baltics represented the tonic of higher risk and profit they needed to balance their slow but low-risk business at home, which tempted them to pursue easy lending policy. Fifth, both the US Federal Reserve system and the ECB exercised very loose monetary policy during this period, instigating a substantial carry trade. Finally, neither Swedish nor Latvian financial regulators did much to rein in the excessive credit expansion.

Banking in Latvia was highly profitable, so why would one hold back? An International Monetary Fund (IMF) report from December 2005 noted: "An additional factor is that exposure of foreign banks' subsidiaries or branches to Latvia represents only a very small share of their total portfolios, while profits derived from this business constitute a far greater fraction of their consolidated profit. This could induce foreign banks to assume greater risk than is beneficial from the Latvian perspective."[5]

The commercial banks were aware of the risks, and in 2007 the two main Swedish banks, Swedbank and SEB, slowed down their credits to Latvia, whereas a relative latecomer, Nordea, compensated somewhat by increasing its market share as late as 2008, and Parex Bank kept up with them.

Banking ownership in Latvia differed significantly from that in the other ten new eastern EU members, where foreign-owned banks held four-fifths of the banking assets; in Latvia, this share was only 60 percent in September 2008, compared with 97 percent in Estonia and 85 percent in Lithuania. As a consequence, Latvia in general, and Parex Bank in particular, was more exposed than its neighbors to the vagaries of the international wholesale banking market, whereas the foreign-owned banks were mainly financed with loans from their parent institutions.[6]

A couple of mitigating factors were at play. During the high inflation in 1991–92, Latvia suffered immense demonetization, and the ratio of credit and money to GDP fell to extreme lows. As late as 2000, Latvia's outstanding credit volume was only 18 percent of GDP, whereas the total credit volume usually approximates GDP in a modern capitalist economy. A long and steady process of remonetization proceeded. Although credit as a share of GDP rose fast, it reached only 88 percent of GDP at the end of 2007 (figure 2.2), which was close to the EU average.[7] Therefore, Latvia could not be described as overleveraged. Moreover, toxic assets such as collateralized debt obligations and other mortgage-based securities were absent.

The high investment ratio, which soared to the extraordinary level of 40 percent of GDP in 2006 and 2007, was reminiscent of the most vibrant East Asian tigers. Much of the investment was financed with capital inflows, but until 2005 the national saving ratio was 23 percent of GDP, which was quite respectable. Yet it fell to 15 percent of GDP in 2007 as cheap money flooded

Figure 2.2 Credit as a share of GDP, 2000–10

percent of GDP

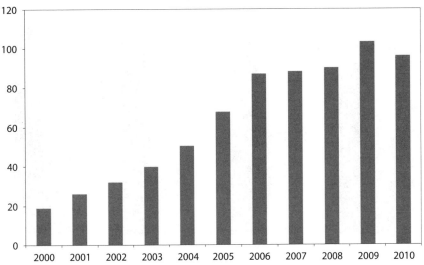

Source: Bank of Latvia, www.bank.lv (accessed on January 24, 2011).

Latvia. The gap between investment (gross capital formation) and the sum of national savings and foreign direct investment grew substantial, peaking at 18 percent of GDP in 2007 (figure 2.3). This gap appears to be the single best predictor of which countries end up in crisis.[8]

Considerable economic imbalances accumulated in the private sector during the boom years. In 2002, Latvia's inflation plunged to a nadir at 1.5 percent and hovered between 1.5 and 3.6 percent a year for the six years before Latvia joined the European Union, but from 2004 it rose to between 6 and 8 percent a year until it took off to double digits in late 2007 (figure 2.4). Annualized inflation (consumer price index [CPI]) peaked at 17.9 percent in May 2008. As a consequence, Latvia was far above the Maastricht limit for inflation of around 3 percent a year, and the country's euro adoption was impossible without major change.

The causes of inflation were multiple, allowing each school of thought to offer its favorite explanation. Latvia started with a low price level, and after it joined the European Union a gradual convergence of prices ensued, which led to higher inflation in Latvia than in wealthier EU countries. Another reason was that the prices of oil and gas, imported from Russia, rose sharply in the years 2004–08.

A third cause of inflation was a tightening labor market. Wage rises were considerably greater than inflation. To a large extent, this reflected the high rise

Figure 2.3 Investment, savings, and foreign direct investment, 2004–07

percent of GDP

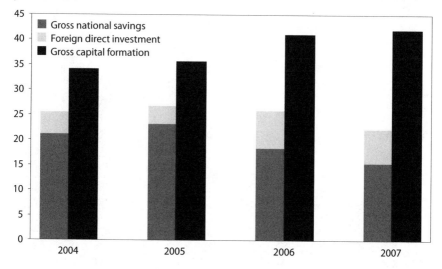

Source: IMF, *World Economic Outlook* database, October 2010, www.imf.org (accessed on November 23, 2010).

in productivity as well as initially depressed real wages, but from 2005 gross wages increased by over 10 percent a year, peaking at an annualized rate of 33 percent in the third quarter of 2007 (figure 2.4). The labor market was tight, especially in the booming construction sector. When Latvia entered the European Union, three old EU members—Sweden, the United Kingdom, and Ireland—opened their labor markets instantly, and noticeable emigration started to the United Kingdom and Ireland. Labor competition from emigration drove up wages on an ever tighter Latvian labor market. For political reasons, it was out of the question to try to ease the shortage of labor via immigration, since ethnic Latvians were happy to have established a clear majority in their own land.

The fourth and dominant cause of the rising inflation was the massive domestic credit expansion. Prices of domestic industries rose much faster than prices of export industries, with construction prices peaking at 30 percent in the first quarter of 2007, which was then four times the CPI (figure 2.4). Real estate prices jumped most of all by more than 60 percent in both 2005 and 2006, skyrocketing by 240 percent from 2003 to 2007.[9]

Unit labor costs had been very low and even fell from 2000 until 2005, as Latvia carried out all the reforms required for EU accession, which greatly improved efficiency. A European Commission report assessed the period 2000–07 thus: "growth accounting analysis shows that catching up in the Baltics was fuelled by [total factor productivity] gains of a size among the largest recorded by emerging economies in recent times and that investment rates were also very sustained and rising until 2007."[10]

Figure 2.4 Consumer price index, gross wages, and construction prices, 2004–10 (percent change over the corresponding period of the previous year)

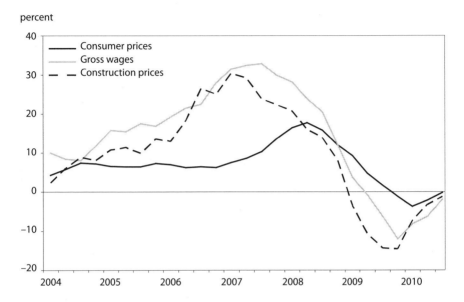

Source: IMF, *World Economic Outlook* database, October 2010, www.imf.org (accessed on November 23, 2010).

But from 2005 until the first quarter of 2008, unit labor costs almost doubled (figure 2.5) and wages in domestic industries rose faster than those in the export industry. This was not a traditional Balassa-Samuelson effect, which implies that in countries that are catching up, productivity rises faster in export industries than domestic industries, but since the labor market is unified, wages increase simultaneously in both sectors, thus rising faster than productivity would justify.[11] An important factor driving the rapid wage increases was free movement of labor in the European Union, providing Latvians with opportunities to seek better-paying jobs in other EU countries.

The real effective exchange rate (REER) did not rise all that much in 2004–06, but in early 2007 wage and price inflation accelerated, undermining competitiveness. Altogether, the CPI-based REER appreciated moderately by 15 percent from 2004 until the end of 2007 (figure 2.6). This was significant but no disaster. From 1999 until 2008, Latvia saw a smaller rise in its REER than the Czech Republic and Slovakia, which hardly experienced any crisis, and far less than Romania (figure 2.7).[12] It is therefore an exaggeration to say that Latvia priced itself out of the export markets, as is often claimed. It is more accurate that excessive capital inflows crowded out manufacturing and export industries. Export competitiveness needed to improve, but it was not unattainable.

Figure 2.5   Unit labor cost, 2000–09

index, 2005=100, seasonally adjusted

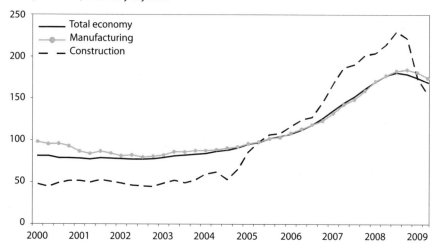

Source: Organization for Economic Cooperation and Development, http://stats.oecd.org (accessed on December 2, 2010).

Figure 2.6   Real effective exchange rate, 2000–10

index, 1999 = 100 (deflator: consumer price indices)

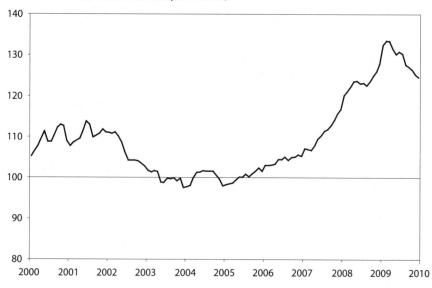

Source: Eurostat database, http://epp.eurostat.ec.europa.eu (accessed on December 3, 2010).

Figure 2.7 Real effective exchange rate growth in Central and Eastern Europe, 1999–2008

index, EU-27 = 100

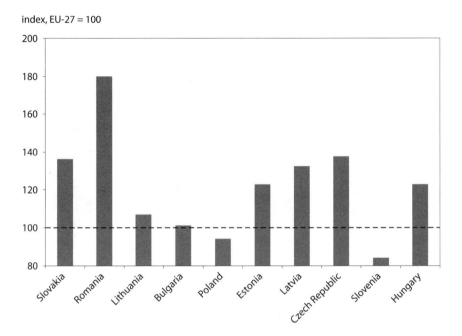

Source: Eurostat database, http://epp.eurostat.ec.europa.eu (accessed on May 27, 2010); authors' calculations.

The expanded credit did not stay at home but boosted imports by 27 to 31 percent a year in 2004–06, though imports started decelerating in 2007, as credit expansion slowed down (figure 2.8). Exports could not keep up with imports, and the current account deficit rose, peaking at 22.5 percent of GDP in 2006–07 and becoming the most alarming precrisis indicator; a current account deficit of 4 to 5 percent of GDP is usually considered the limit for financial health. Long-term foreign direct investment amounted to only 4 to 8 percent of GDP (figure 2.9). As a consequence, Latvia piled up a large external debt, which reached 128 percent of GDP in 2007 in gross terms, but this was largely private debt, and the net external debt was only 50 percent of GDP (figure 2.10).

The least concern was public finances. The government regularly planned for a small budget deficit, but with growth persistently higher than anticipated during these years, revenues were also larger. Even after supplementary expenditure increases, the country had a budget deficit of barely 1 percent of GDP every year (figure 2.11), although real expenditures grew by 80 percent from 2003 to 2007. The public debt was minuscule at 9 percent of GDP at the end of 2007 (figure 2.12).

Figure 2.8   Annual growth in imports, 2004–07

percent, year over year

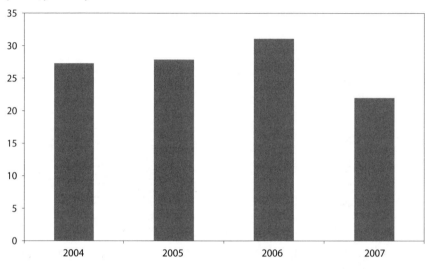

Source: Central Statistical Bureau of Latvia, www.csb.gov.lv (accessed on November 24, 2010).

Figure 2.9   Current account deficit and foreign direct investment, 2004–07

percent of GDP

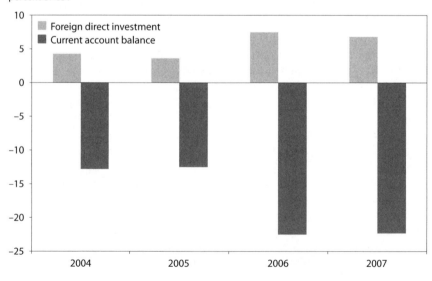

Source: Bank of Latvia, www.bank.lv (accessed on November 24, 2010).

Figure 2.10 Gross and net foreign debt, 2004–07

percent of GDP

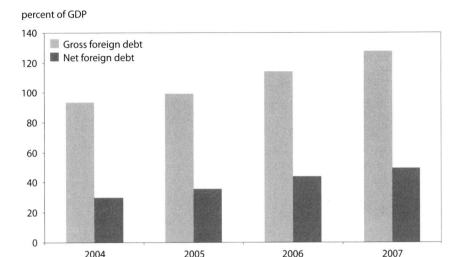

Source: Bank of Latvia, www.bank.lv (accessed on November 24, 2010).

The Latvian overheating was no surprise. It was evident for anybody who wanted to see it. And the IMF did. Since 2005, it had warned clearly and persistently. An IMF note after a staff visit to Latvia in late 2005 said it all:

> ...current growth is outpacing the economy's capacity to generate goods and services... price and wage inflation have increased and the external current account deficit has widened. Inflation, moreover, is likely to remain above the Maastricht threshold for some time, implying that euro adoption will be delayed....
>
> Bursts of very high growth will frustrate, rather than support, Latvia's goal of sustained income convergence. Rapid wage and price increases that are not backed by productivity improvements will erode external competitiveness and further widen the current account deficit. Credit that serves to boost consumption and real estate will not expand the economy's long-term potential or generate the resources to repay debt.[13]

Consequently, the IMF recommended that the Latvian authorities "take early action to contain overheating pressures," but little could be done. With a fixed exchange rate and free capital movements, Latvia was caught in the so-called impossible trinity, which meant that it could not pursue an independent monetary policy.[14] Formally, the Bank of Latvia set interest rates, but because of the quasi currency board system interest rates were market determined, and Latvia had hardly any bonds.

Figure 2.11   Budget balance, 2004–07

percent of GDP

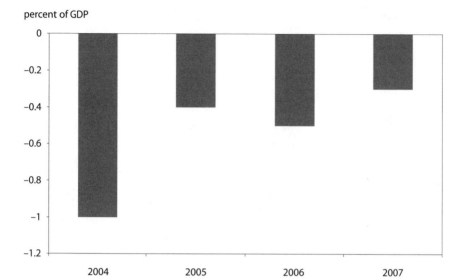

Source: Central Statistical Bureau of Latvia, www.csb.gov.lv (accessed on November 2, 2010).

Figure 2.12   Public debt, 2004–07

percent of GDP

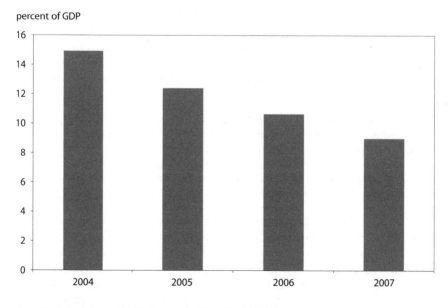

Source: Bank of Latvia, www.bank.lv (accessed on November 24, 2010).

In 2004–07, the ECB pursued an expansionary monetary policy, with large expansion of the money supply, just like the US Federal Reserve. International investors developed large-scale carry trade of cheap international credits to Eastern Europe in general and to Latvia in particular. The ECB only targeted inflation and harbored no apparent concern about growing asset bubbles or the risk of financial instability.

The Latvian authorities had mainly two means at hand, fiscal policy and bank regulation. With its double-digit growth rate in 2005–07, Latvia should have maintained a persistent budget surplus of a few percent of GDP, as Estonia and Bulgaria did. In the midst of the boom, however, this was not very popular, while the government was rather populist. Latvian society was caught in euphoria. Both tax revenues and GDP growth persistently exceeded forecasts, eliminating planned budget deficits. After every summer, however, the government produced a supplementary budget that raised public expenditures by a couple of percent of GDP, thus eating up the revenue windfall and causing a tiny budget deficit. Bankers, businessmen, consumers, and government alike felt that the boom disproved all the warnings they had heard since 2004, which rendered the eventual crisis all the more devastating. Still, Estonia faced a pretty severe financial crisis in spite of a very conservative fiscal policy.

The other option was bank regulation, which offered a range of opportunities. The Bank of Latvia did raise the required reserve ratios of the commercial banks repeatedly, starting as early as 2005, but more could have been done. Mortgage loans could have been restricted as a share of the total price but were not. Limits on credit expansion could have been considered.[15] Bank credits could have been reined in and channeled from consumption and real estate to production. But bank regulation could not have been taken very far, because the Latvian economy was small and completely open, so Latvian banking operations could easily have moved to another country. The Swedish Riksbank and the Financial Supervisory Authority (Finansinspektionen) should also have paid attention to the excessive exposure of the Swedish commercial banks to the Baltic economies, but they did nothing.

A third measure, however, should have been used: taxation. Astoundingly, individuals who speculated in real estate did not have to pay any tax on their gains if they held their property for at least one year. Similarly, no capital gains tax existed, and it should have been introduced. Nor did Latvia have any property tax on residential buildings (only on land), but it was introduced during the crisis. All these taxes would have helped to cool down the speculation and thus impede real estate inflation. The IMF proposed wage controls, but they had hardly been possible, because the labor market was truly tight, and the free-market mentality objected to such interference in the market. Wage increases were driven by the market and not by trade unions.[16]

An European Commission report offers a vivid description of the overheating:

> By 2007, the overheating reached its peak. Large current account deficits were compounded by new types of vulnerability. Galloping private credit, mostly

in euro, was increasingly financing a housing bubble, heightening the bottle-necks and distortion on the supply side of the economy, including in terms of available skilled workforce and products. Financing to the private sector was increasingly dependent on a small group of common (foreign) lenders, dominantly Scandinavian banks, who themselves were increasingly dependent on market financing. At the same time, domestic banks (most notably Parex Bank in Latvia) at the zenith of the global financial crisis experienced major difficulties with rolling over their foreign loans in the face of extreme exposure to the housing sector.[17]

The government was content with the boom and told the European Union and the IMF alike: "Our budget deficit is below 3 percent of GDP. What do you want from us?" The essence of the Maastricht criteria, however, is that the budget has to be balanced during the economic cycle, and during periods of stagnation or recession, the budget deficit should not exceed 3 percent of GDP. Some regulatory restrictions on credits were introduced in the spring of 2007, as well as some quantitative limits on how large a share of collateral a bank could lend and some limits on the size of the loan in relation to official income, but it was already too late.

Politics of Complacency

To understand Latvian policymaking, one needs to consider the Latvian polit-ical party structure and leading politicians. The governments in this period were relaxed and phlegmatic. They were invariably coalitions of three to five center-right parties. The party system evolved over time with various parties forming blocs. Around this time, five dominant political blocs emerged. The parliamen-tary elections of 100 members in October 2006 showed their relative strength.

Four were mainly ethnically Latvian center-right parties. Three—People's Party, Latvia's First Party/Latvia's Way, and the Union of Greens and Farmers—were considered "oligarchic" parties, formed around one major businessman, who was not always the official political leader. They participated in almost every government coalition. Their personal interests differentiated them.

People's Party was founded in 1998 by Andris Šķēle, a leading busi-nessman, who was prime minister in 1995–97 and again in 1999–2000. He left the party chairmanship to Atis Slakteris, who held different ministerial port-folios. Aigars Kalvītis was another party leader. With 23 of the parliament's 100 seats after the 2006 parliamentary elections, it was the biggest party.

Its close competitor was Latvia's First Party/Latvia's Way. Since November 2007 Ainārs Šlesers, another prominent businessman, has been its chairman. Ivars Godmanis, Latvia's first prime minister in 1990–93, originally one of the leaders of Latvia's Popular Front, belonged to this party. It obtained only 10 seats in the 2006 elections.

The third oligarchic party was the Union of Greens and Farmers. It was a provincial party, uniting Latvian farmers and people in small towns, but its informal leader was Aivars Lembergs, the long-time mayor of the port city Ventspils.[18] In 2006, he was charged with corruption, money laundering, and abuse of public office, but his complex court case is still ongoing.[19] Both Lembergs and his party have kept a lower political profile than the other two establishment parties. It held 18 seats after the 2006 elections.

The fourth center-right party was New Era, formed in 2002 by Einars Repše, who had governed the Bank of Latvia for a decade. It gathered young political outsiders and professionals, focusing on combating corruption. In the 2006 elections, it received 18 seats.

In 2005, several mainly ethnically Russian groups merged into Harmony Center. Its chairman was the young Russian Nils Ušakovs and the leader of its parliamentary faction was ethnically Latvian Jānis Urbanovičs. In the 2006 elections, it gained 17 seats, one less than the Union of Farmers and Greens as well as New Era.

The parliament of 2006 also included For Human Rights in United Latvia, a smaller Russian nationalist party, and For Fatherland and Freedom, a small Latvian nationalist party, both of which played only marginal roles. Latvian politicians have a habit of abandoning their parties and setting up new parties, but increasingly the party system is being consolidated.

The coalition governments in Latvia have changed almost every year. In the 2002 parliamentary elections, New Era won the most seats in parliament, and Repše became prime minister and one of us (Valdis Dombrovskis) minister of finance. However, this coalition government fell apart when the prime minister attacked specific members of his coalition for corruption, and he resigned in February 2004.

In March 2004, another center-right coalition was formed under Indulis Emsis of the Union of Greens and Farmers, but he had to resign when the parliament refused to accept his budget. In December 2004, Aigars Kalvītis of People's Party became prime minister with a similar coalition. New Era joined his government in late 2004, but in April 2006 the New Era ministers resigned because of Kalvītis's unwillingness to act on a major corruption scandal in Jurmala, the seaside resort outside Riga.[20]

Kalvītis stayed on, the first prime minister in the history of post-Soviet Latvia to have his government reelected in the parliamentary elections in 2006. Still, he was haunted by accusations by the independent Corruption Prevention and Combating Bureau (KNAB), for violating campaign financing rules during People's Party's 2006 parliamentary election campaign. In December 2007, he was forced to resign because he attempted to fire the head of KNAB, which prompted popular protests—the so-called umbrella revolution.[21] His government had lasted three years, although its composition changed twice, but it had done little to fend off the coming financial crisis.

Notes

1. Servaas Deroose, Elena Flores, Gabriele Giudice, and Alessandro Turrini, "The Tale of the Baltics: Experiences, Challenges Ahead and Main Lessons," ECFIN Economic Brief, no. 10 (European Commission, July 2010, 8).

2. The Treaty on the Functioning of the European Union, *Official Journal of the European Union C 115/108-9*, May 9, 2008, Article 140; Michael Marrese, "The Convergence of CEEMEA Countries as the Global Recession Ends," JPMorgan, New York, July 29, 2009; European Union, "Acceding Countries and ERM-II," EFC/ECFIN/109/03 (Athens, April 5, 2003).

3. A large literature has accurately analyzed this credit boom before it broke, notably, Morris Goldstein, "Emerging-Market Financial Crises: Lessons and Prospects" (speech at the 2007 Annual Meeting, Institute of International Finance, Washington, October 20, 2007); Philip R. Lane and Gian Maria Milesi-Ferretti, "Capital Flows to Central and Eastern Europe," *Emerging Markets Review* 8, no. 2 (2007): 106–23; Susan Schadler, "Are Large External Imbalances in Central Europe Sustainable?" in *Challenges of Globalization: Imbalances and Growth*, eds. Anders Åslund and Marek Dabrowski (Washington: Peterson Institute for International Economics, 2008).

4. The Cabinet of Ministers of the Republic of Latvia, "Transcript of the Meeting of Prime Minister of the Republic of Latvia Valdis Dombrovskis with the Representatives of the International Mass Media on Monday, March 23, 2009," State Chancellery, March 27, 2009, www.mk.gov.lv (accessed on December 7, 2010).

5. "Aide-Mémoire: IMF Staff Visit to the Republic of Latvia, November 30-December 2, 2005," International Monetary Fund, undated.

6. International Monetary Fund, Republic of Latvia, "Request for Stand-By Arrangement," December 19, 2008, p. 7, www.imf.org (accessed on November 15, 2010).

7. Bas B. Bakker and Anne-Marie Gulde, "The Credit Boom in the EU New Member States: Bad Luck or Bad Policies?" IMF Working Paper 10/130 (Washington: International Monetary Fund, 2010, 15).

8. Zsolt Darvas and Jean Pisani-Ferry, "Avoiding a New European Divide," Bruegel Policy Brief 10 (Brussels: Bruegel, December 2008).

9. Bakker and Gulde, "The Credit Boom in the EU New Member States," 19.

10. Deroose, Flores, Giudice, and Turrini, "The Tale of the Baltics," 12.

11. We owe this point to Bas Bakker.

12. Bakker and Gulde, "The Credit Boom in the EU New Member States," 35.

13. "Aide-Mémoire: IMF Staff Visit to the Republic of Latvia."

14. Lars Oxelheim, *International Financial Integration* (Heidelberg: Springer Verlag Berlin, 1990).

15. "Aide-Mémoire: IMF Staff Visit to the Republic of Latvia."

16. Valdis Dombrovskis, "Dilemma: palielināt algas un... inflācija" ["Dilemma: Increase of Salaries and...Inflation"], *Latvijas Avize*, April 3, 2007.

17. Deroose, Flores, Giudice, and Turrini, "The Tale of the Baltics," 5.

18. DELFI, "ZZS un Lemberga partija saskaņos augstu amatpersonu un valsts uzņēmumu vadī bas kandidātus" ["Union of Greens and Farmers Will Agree with Lembergs' Party on Potential Appointees to High State Positions and Corporations"], July 14, 2010.

19. "Bribery Allegations Against Lembergs Spark Rumours of Widespread Graft in Parliament," *Baltic Times*, March 21, 2007.

20. Freedom House, *Freedom in the World—Latvia* (Freedom in the World Report, Washington, 2007), www.freedomhouse.org (accessed on April 6, 2011).

21. Alexandru Rusu, *Latvia* (report, Civil Society Against Corruption, September 2010), www. againstcorruption.eu (accessed on April 6, 2011).

3

Policy Choices and the Program of Crisis Resolution, 2008

In 2008, Latvia entered the bust of a classical boom-bust cycle.[1] Latvia had already begun to feel the heat from the global financial crisis in early 2007 through the restriction of credit. With less credit, housing prices started falling and with them both consumer demand and investment. Output contracted so sharply by the second quarter of 2008 that it threatened the banks. With the bankruptcy of Lehman Brothers in September 2008, liquidity froze throughout the world, and Latvia, which heavily depended on foreign finance, faced a "sudden stop."

In the absence of international liquidity, Parex Bank—Latvia's second largest bank and largest independent commercial bank—collapsed in November 2008. It had run into problems due to the global financial crisis and mismanagement by its former owners. The government had to nationalize and recapitalize it. The costs were so sizable that the government was compelled to call in the International Monetary Fund (IMF) and the European Commission for emergency financing. The government concluded a Stand-By Arrangement with the IMF, which was reinforced with even more financing from the European Commission and Nordic countries.

The financial crisis was already evident in late 2007, although its severity was not. During that period Latvia was forced to change governments because Prime Minister Aigar Kalvītis was embroiled in a scandal for attempting to fire the head of the Corruption Prevention and Combating Bureau (KNAB), which prompted the "umbrella revolution" against him.[2] After negotiations, the same parties agreed to form a "crisis" government in December 2007 but with Ivars Godmanis as prime minister. Having been Latvia's first prime minister after the country regained independence, Godmanis was, on the one hand, generally respected both in Latvia and abroad. He was a big man with a white beard, exuding natural authority. On the other hand, he was also controversial because many people associated his government with the lawlessness, corruption, messy privatization, and economic hardship of the immediate post-Soviet period, and he represented the oligarchic Latvia's First Party/Latvia's Way.[3]

In the fall of 2008, four officials dominated the Latvian political scene. One was Godmanis, and the others were Minister of Finance Atis Slakteris, Governor of the Bank of Latvia Ilmārs Rimšēvičs, and President Valdis Zatlers. In almost every regard, Slakteris seemed the opposite of Godmanis. He was seen as the ultimate party politician, with little apparent understanding of economics or finance. He was usually the last to suggest austerity measures.

Rimšēvičs has been governor of the Bank of Latvia since December 2001, when Einars Repše quit to return to politics. He was Repše's deputy at the Bank of Latvia but acted strictly as the bank's governor. He stood for three firm ideas: fixed exchange rate, early entry of Latvia into the Economic and Monetary Union, and therefore a tight budget to fulfill the Maastricht criteria.

Zatlers became president in July 2007, elected by the parliament. He was in most regards a political outsider, not belonging to any party, though he had been a member of the board of the Latvian Popular Front in 1988–89, and he enjoyed high professional status as the country's star surgeon. Since Latvia is a parliamentary republic, presidential powers are limited. The president appoints the prime minister to be confirmed by a parliamentary majority and has the right to call a referendum on the dissolution of the parliament, but if the people say no, he is forced to resign. Zatlers played an active role in the financial crisis. He complained about the failure of the government, reflecting public discontent, and toyed with the idea of early elections, but he also tried to mobilize support for the policy of the government of which he was often critical.

Fall 2008: The Bubble Pops

The global financial crisis started when US real estate prices began declining in the second half of 2006. In 2007, Latvia, one of the most overheated economies in the world by then, was among the first countries to be stung by the crisis. Initially, few understood the severity of the crisis, and strong business interests held their own within the government. Yet, one of the most insightful and critical economic observers, Lars Christensen of Danske Bank, warned in July 2008: "There is a risk that the unwinding of imbalances can lead to an 'output loss' of 10–15% of GDP in the Baltic states, Bulgaria and Romania."[4] The blows were several and hard but spread over two years. Five big, distinct blows set off the crisis, and they were all financial.

First, the Latvian authorities initiated an anti-inflation plan in early 2007. The Bank of Latvia continued tightening its regulatory policies, primarily by restricting mortgage lending and increasing reserve ratios. Unlike previous minor reserve tightening, this policy had some impact, and lending started decelerating in mid-2007.

Second, more or less simultaneously, in the summer of 2007, SEB began tightening its credit policies toward Latvia and a few months later so did Swedbank. The peak of the credit boom thus ended, initially hitting the housing and construction sectors. Housing prices fell at a rate of 35 percent a year from the second quarter of 2007, becoming the driver of the downturn. Latvia faced a full-blown credit crunch from the beginning of 2008. Economic growth slowed, as consumption and investment fell. Growth was negligible in the first quarter of 2008, and output declined in the second quarter. Even so, inflation peaked at 17.9 percent in May 2008. Wage growth decelerated and employment declined in the early fall of 2008. By the third quarter, Latvia's GDP approached free fall.

The third blow was the Lehman Brothers bankruptcy on September 15, 2008, when Latvia was already deep into a financial crisis. Even so, it hit Latvia with a "sudden stop." Global liquidity froze, shutting off the country's access to international financial markets over night.[5] An already severe recession became a rampant financial crisis.

Fourth, the prime victim of the sudden stop was Parex Bank, the biggest domestically owned Latvian bank, with one-fifth of all bank assets in the country. It could no longer finance itself on the European wholesale market, and it had syndicated loans falling due. A run on its deposits started, and it lost one-quarter of its deposits from the end of August through November. The government had no choice but to take over. On November 8, 2008, the Latvian government announced it was buying 51 percent of Parex Bank from its owners Viktors Krasovickis and Valerijs Kargins for the symbolic amount of 2 lats. Yet, the outflow of deposits did not stop. On December 1, the authorities imposed a partial freeze on deposit withdrawals to conserve liquidity. The government had to recapitalize Parex at a total of 4.9 percent of GDP, and 2.6 percent of GDP was needed in additional guarantees.[6]

Fifth, Latvia had no access to international or European liquidity, although it was a member of the European Union and as such a shareholder of the European Central Bank (ECB). It had little choice but to go to the IMF. As Jean Pisani-Ferry and Adam S. Posen write: "The euro did little to improve the crisis response of neighboring countries in Central and Eastern Europe.... Even if the formal mandates of the [ECB] and the Eurogroup...do not formally include it, broader stability in the region should be a major economic and political objective as well."[7] The little liquidity that was made available stemmed from the Swedish banks, and the Swedish Riksbank and the Danish central bank offered a bridge loan to keep Latvia going until the IMF-EU-Nordic package was concluded. Another source of finance was the European Investment Bank (EIB), an EU institution, which concluded an agreement with Latvia on a credit of €750 million on October 30, 2008, for EU funds cofinancing, in the early stages of the crisis.[8]

To understand the political economy of the Latvian financial crisis, it is crucial to closely follow the events that unfolded. It is always striking how unaware most actors seem in a financial crisis until it is a reality. Late Professor

Rudiger Dornbusch used to say that a financial crisis usually happens much later than anybody expected, but when it starts everything goes much faster than anybody could have imagined.

Although financial experts, bankers, and Prime Minister Godmanis were aware of the impending crisis in the first half of 2008, little worth mentioning happened in economic policy. The first scare of financial crisis occurred in February 2008 when the exchange rate suffered a speculative attack. It was instigated at the street level with runs on the foreign exchange kiosks. This attempt failed, and that's possibly why Latvians were not so worried about devaluation later on. As late as March 2008, Latvia managed to sell €400 million of Eurobonds due in 2018 at a decent yield of 5.5 percent.[9] In the summer of 2008, rumors circulated about possible bank failures, pinpointing the big Swedish banks.

Absurdly, in August 2008 Latvia held two referendums on unrelated issues—one on early parliamentary elections and another on raising minimal pensions to the existential minimum. Both failed, but even so pensions were raised through indexation and supplementary pensions. Following several scandals, confidence in the government was low, and opinion polls from October 2008 indicated that none of the four government parties would have passed the 5 percent threshold to be represented in parliament. The beneficiaries were the two big opposition parties, Harmony Center and New Era.

The first serious calls for austerity emerged at the end of September 2008. Godmanis led the charge and ordered state agencies to prepare for a cut in their staff of 10 percent and warned that the salaries of state employees would not be raised in 2009. Trade unions refused to accept any freezing of state salaries, and an opinion poll in early October claimed that 63 percent of the population concurred. The union turned to the parliament after failing to persuade the government. The police threatened to strike, and farmers were upset over the government wanting to cut agricultural subsidies. In late October, more than 1,000 medical staff went on strike demanding higher salaries.[10] Austerity was still a distant goal.

The initial budget proposal of October 6, 2008, forecast a budget deficit of 1.85 percent of GDP, on the basis of expected GDP growth of 2 percent in 2009, inflation of 7.6 percent, and unemployment of 8.1 percent. Bank of Latvia Governor Rimšēvičs protested that the real deficit would be 4 to 5.5 percent of GDP, as GDP was not likely to grow. In fact the IMF warned in October that GDP in 2009 would fall by 2.2 percent. Finance Minister Slakteris did not participate in the discussion of the budget because he was abroad on holiday.[11]

The public discussion, however, soon turned, when in October and early November 2008 negative statistics started dripping in. On October 14, 2008, Eurostat announced that Latvia's industrial production in August had plummeted by 11.1 percent.[12] In October, retail sales plummeted by 14.4 percent, showing that domestic demand was plunging because of lack of liquidity.[13]

The number of enterprises going bankrupt surged. Unemployment rose fast and reached 7.2 percent in November.[14]

These statistics aggravated the public's perception of the economy, reinforcing the crisis mood. Latvians no longer opposed cuts but called for more radical austerity measures. Public demands for benefits gave way to political and social groups demanding that fat cats be punished—the president's chancery, state officials, the parliament, state corporations, and local governments. Prime Minister Godmanis (not the minister of finance) had already started cutting state wages from early October. One "sacred cow" after the other was slaughtered with great speed, and after every slaughter the public cried for more. The austerity campaign acquired an almost revolutionary zeal. Most controversial was eliminating the substantial fees that many senior officials received for being members of boards of state corporations, which made up about half their income, and the parliament's decision to abolish all these fees barely scraped through.[15] Since becoming a member of the North Atlantic Treaty Organization (NATO) in 2004, Latvia had firmly endeavored to spend 2 percent of GDP on its defense. Now, for the first time, the government was determined to cut military expenditures.[16] Eventually, they were trimmed to 1 percent of GDP.

On November 7, 2008, ironically the anniversary of Russia's October revolution, Latvia suffered a big blow. Initial statistics indicated that GDP in the third quarter of 2008 had fallen by 4.2 percent (later revised to 4.7 percent). It dawned on the Latvian elite that their economy was near free fall. The tone of the public discourse changed further. GDP forecasts for 2009 were revised nearly daily. On November 3, the European Commission predicted a fall of 2.7 percent. In late November, Swedbank foresaw a contraction of 4 percent, followed by SEB predicting a decline of 5 percent, which was also the IMF's revised December forecast and became the basis for its financing program. Sensibly, Minister of Economy Kaspars Gerhards observed that the GDP for the next year could not possibly be forecast.[17]

The public urged the government to act to escape the crisis, complaining that it took baby steps and shielded vested interests. The chairman of the Association of Realtors demanded that the government aim for a budget surplus of 5 percent of GDP. One liberal opposition politician, Aigars Štokenbergs, called the budget "turbid and helpless." A survey of businessmen showed that 54 percent wanted a balanced or surplus budget. The Free Trade Union Confederation of Latvia joined this choir, complaining that the government's budget was overoptimistic and did not consider the social partners' proposals on expenditure cuts.[18]

On November 14, the parliament adopted a budget for 2009, with a slight majority of 53 to 43. New Era and Harmony Center opposed it as insufficient and unrealistic, but this budget was perceived as temporary.[19] All knew that its assumptions were excessively optimistic, and Godmanis declared that he would cut public expenditures ad hoc. On November 24, all state bonuses and other additional expenditures for 2009 were eliminated.

Besides negative statistics, false analogies were also in the news. From mid-October, various international analysts claimed that Latvia was becoming another Iceland, where three big banks had been just nationalized, and that the same economic problems were likely to emerge in Latvia. Godmanis responded that an Icelandic scenario was impossible in Latvia. In particular, Iceland's ratio of banking assets to GDP was several times larger than that in Latvia.[20] He should also have added that Iceland had a floating exchange rate and very high interest rates and was not a member of the European Union.

The crisis also subjected the Latvian government to sniping from within. A typical news report read: "In the corridors of the parliament the question is intensely discussed when the Godmanis government will fall." It was predicted to fall in the spring before the local elections.[21] And sure enough, the government fell in February 2009. Representatives of the coalition party, the People's Party, suggested repeatedly that their leader Andris Šķēle should become prime minister once again. Šķēle exploited the drama of crisis but fudged his response, claiming that the three tasks of the Latvian economy were: "Productivity, productivity and once again productivity."[22] He thus paraphrased one of Vladimir Lenin's most famous statements but said nothing about how to take Latvia out of the crisis. On another occasion, he complained that the budget for 2009 was too optimistic, requiring sharp correction, but abstained from revealing the change he had in mind.[23] Clearly, Šķēle sought the moment to become prime minister again.

President Zatlers also kept criticizing the Godmanis government. He said that he was ready for the possible resignation of the government but added that a change of government in the midst of such a difficult economic situation would be undesirable.[24] Soon afterward, he proposed a referendum on the dissolution of the parliament but complained that a change of parliament would take too long—five months—and desired a better constitutional order.[25] The president even blamed one specific party, People's Party, for Latvia's poor preparation for the financial crisis.[26] Speaking about Slakteris, Zatlers said: "It would be good if we could raise the prestige of the minister of finance."[27] His frequent public criticism undermined the government. Evidently, he reckoned that Latvia needed firmer hands at the rudder, though his criticism was directed against the ministers of finance and economy rather than the prime minister.

Most clouds have a silver lining, and even Latvia's dark clouds in the last quarter of 2008 showed flickers of hope. After peaking in May 2008, annualized inflation fell like a stone by about one percentage point a month, and foreign trade was turning around. As domestic demand contracted, exports increased, rising by no less than 14 percent during the first nine months of 2008, while imports declined by 1.6 percent. The large current account deficit shrank in no time.[28] An early structural reform was per-student financing of education, providing state financing in relation to the number of students, which the trade unions accepted as a means of redirecting funding to teachers.

Run on Parex Bank: Latvia Calls in the IMF

Rather than calming the public mood, the adoption of the 2009 budget was seen by the public as a declaration of the government's impotence. On November 15, the deposit run on Parex Bank turned into a run to exchange lats for euros and other foreign currencies. Rumors were rife that devaluation of the lat was imminent. Slakteris hardly helped by declaring that the lat was stable: "Even if the whole world economy collapses, the lat will be the last to fall."[29]

The Bank of Latvia reacted to the deposit withdrawals by increasing liquidity, extending domestic credit, and easing reserve ratios, which reduced its foreign exchange reserves by one-quarter during the three months from September to November 2008. Like other new EU members, Latvia had relatively small reserves compared with its short-term external debt.[30]

Therefore, it could not take the easing of its monetary policy far. Yet, contrary to widespread fears, Latvia did not experience any financial meltdown or another severe bank run. During the height of the liquidity crisis, from the end of August until the end of November 2008, total bank deposits declined by 10 percent excluding valuation effects.[31] The payments system continued to function. As usual late in their assessments, the three rating agencies downgraded Latvia in the fourth quarter of 2008.

The Latvian government was understandably at a loss facing the Parex Bank crisis, so it called in a technical IMF mission in mid-November. Soon the depth of the crisis became evident, and the Latvian authorities requested an IMF Stand-By Arrangement. The first round of the IMF negotiations took place on November 17–23, with Christoph Rosenberg as mission chief.

On November 20, the Latvian security police arrested a Latvian newspaper journalist and a musician for spreading destabilization rumors about the devaluation of the lat. At the same time the security police appealed to the media to not create panic and to publish only properly checked data. These actions stopped short of censorship but violated normal democratic standards.

In early December, all realized how serious the crisis was. Godmanis no longer minced his words but reminded the population that the Latvian GDP had slumped by 37 percent after the collapse of the Soviet Union.[32] He complained that it was difficult to make any plans when the GDP forecasts changed virtually every day. Presciently, the Latvian employment authority warned that unemployment could rise to 15 to 20 percent in 2009.[33] Godmanis declared that international financing was needed for three reasons: to manage Parex Bank, to finance the budget deficit, and to stabilize the financial market. The IMF mission returned to Latvia for negotiations from December 5 to 18. On December 5, Prime Minister Godmanis presented the IMF program to the parliament. A week of intense political negotiations ensued.

At the center of the crisis lay the collapse of Parex Bank. The two owners—Krasovickis and Kargins—were known and well-connected Latvian citizens, who had won the first private license in the Soviet Union to trade in hard currency in

1990. It was one of the early, highly entrepreneurial post-Soviet banks, complete with all the baggage. In 1992, Parex advertised: "We exchange all currencies and ask no questions." In 2005, it announced that Riga was closer to Moscow than Switzerland was and that everyone at Parex spoke Russian. In a last daring blitz, its billboards in Stockholm offered 6.5 percent a year deposit rates in Swedish kronor.[34] Latvians were divided in their views of the two former owners, long the richest men in Latvia. While some were proud of these self-made Latvians who could compete with big foreign banks, others were not. Parex Bank eventually sued the two men in 2010 for "violation of the bank's interests."[35]

Latvia's starting point was that devaluation was unthinkable. The only Latvian official who wavered was Slakteris, stating: "I talked with the executive director of the IMF and he assumed that for the stabilization of the economy the Bank of Latvia has to reduce the exchange rate of the lat. Then we could exit the crisis according to the Argentine scenario: this is already widely discussed by Fund experts. Such a plunge as now, Latvia can never survive." Godmanis instantly rebuked Slakteris and clarified that devaluation was out of the question.[36]

Godmanis contemplated large cuts in public expenditures, slashing state salaries by 40 to 45 percent and reducing staff by 20 percent in certain state institutions.[37] He ordered the state secretaries to assess the possibility of cutting salaries in the state administration by 10 to 30 percent as well as wages in state-owned enterprises by 15 percent. Virtually all public expenditures apart from pensions and social support for the poorest were to be cut.

Yet the government insisted on reducing the flat personal income tax from 25 to 23 percent, while it accepted the IMF demand to raise both the value-added tax (VAT) from 18 to 21 percent and some excise taxes. The corporate profit tax remained at 15 percent.

On December 10, Godmanis gathered social partners to consult about the anticrisis program. The Latvian Confederation of Employers opposed the increased VAT and demanded lower personal income taxes as in Estonia and Lithuania. The Free Trade Union Confederation of Latvia was still more critical: "The draconian tax reform and wage cuts lead to an even more profound crisis and undermine the basis of the state—the economy and enterprise. They lead also to increased unemployment and reduced demand." They threatened to contest the new laws in the Constitutional Court. Thus both employers and trade unions refused to accept the government's austerity plan, but Godmanis did not compromise.[38]

Needless to say, the opposition had no reason to go soft on the government, demanding a more radical austerity program. Their anger was directed against the old elite of top officials living in symbiosis with wealthy businessmen while claiming to defend the poor and pensioners. On December 10, the two main opposition parties, New Era and Harmony Center, demanded the resignation of the Godmanis government. Harmony Center's parliamentary leader Jānis Urbanovičs complained that there "exists a non-competitive political system with an unchanging political top. All our parties for the last

15 years...are only different pieces of one political 'sausage,' and they differ only by weight and label."[39]

Harmony Center called for a coalition of national unity or national salvation, trying to exploit the situation to become a legitimate government partner. To that effect, it actually signed an agreement in support of the stabilization plan. Characteristic of the public mood, Harmony Center approved of the public salary cuts but complained that the government had not utilized all options to cut the expenditures of the state apparatus.[40]

New Era had called for austerity and anticorruption measures for years. It had no reason to approve of this belated stabilization program, which was softer than New Era desired and contained tax increases. It demanded more professionalism, determination, and transparency, also calling for a government of national unity comprising all the parliamentary parties. It voted against the stabilization program. Representing the hardest liberal opposition to the government's stabilization program, Aigars Štokenbergs criticized it for being too soft on the elite: "Godmanis found tens of reasons not to end tax holidays for dividends, not to introduce capital gains tax and not to tax magnificent villas..., where those 'spoilt by the fat years' built their castles. This government defends only the rich, who need endless tax holidays."[41]

In the midst of this sensitive situation, Minister of Finance Slakteris gave a long interview to Bloomberg television on December 8, 2008, attracting immense public attention. Not exactly fluent in English, Slakteris missed the meaning of many questions and had little to say. The final nail in his political coffin came when he was asked what had led Latvia into such a terrible crisis. He responded with a smile: "Nothing special." This became the slogan of a burgeoning protest movement against the government with posters and t-shirts saying "nothing special." This interview seriously undermined public confidence in the government. The opposition called a vote of no confidence in the minister of finance, which took place on December 11. New Era, Harmony Center, and various independents voted for his ouster with 41 votes, while the government mobilized 53 votes in his defense.[42] But the Godmanis government was doomed.

The public sense of crisis had become profound and all embracing. The ultimate issue was Latvia's national survival. Harmony Center's Urbanovičs exclaimed: "Is there any alternative today to our proposals? Unfortunately, there is one and that is a catastrophic alternative, namely Latvia's ultimate loss of economic independence, its depopulation and the marginalization of the remaining population. People will simply spread out over the world...."[43]

On December 11, the parliament adopted the controversial package of tax changes demanded by the IMF, and the Ministry of Finance published "Latvia's Economic Stabilization and Growth Revival Program." The brief stabilization program set out the basic policies agreed with the IMF and the European Commission.[44] The budget deficit would be 5 percent of GDP in 2009. The total fiscal tightening was assessed at 1 billion lats or 7 percent of GDP in 2009. The public expenditure cuts were draconian: reducing public employees by 15 percent, public nominal wages by 15 percent, and state procurement of goods and services by 25 percent. VAT was to rise by 3 percentage points, and excise duties were to be raised for fuel, coffee, alcohol, and other beverages. At the same time, structural reforms were to be promoted to make the labor market more elastic and facilitate investment.

The International Assistance Package

In December 2008, the IMF, the European Commission, and several European—mainly Nordic—countries prepared and financed an international loan package for Latvia. The stabilization program was concluded as a traditional IMF Stand-By Arrangement on December 18, 2008.[45] It was supposed to last 27 months, and the IMF offered an exceptionally large credit of €1.7 billion or $2.35 billion. The credit was heavily frontloaded with one-third being issued in the first of ten tranches. The IMF Executive Board adopted this program on December 23, only four days after it was concluded. Thus, the first tranche could be disbursed as a Christmas present to badly suffering Latvia.

The IMF led the negotiations, with staff from the European Commission, the European Central Bank (ECB), the World Bank, the European Bank for Reconstruction and Development (EBRD), the Swedish Ministry of Finance, the Riksbank, and other Nordic governments participating. Rarely has an IMF negotiation involved so many participants, and seldom have the views expressed at the table been so varied on the key issue of principle, namely the exchange rate policy. The IMF mission itself had 11 people.[46] It was led by Christoph Rosenberg, who accepted the Latvian argument for maintaining the peg to the euro, but most of his mission was skeptical. The Latvian team was led by Prime Minister Godmanis, Minister of Finance Slakteris, and Bank of Latvia Governor Rimšēvičs. It represented the strong Latvian consensus: maintain the peg at the price that is necessary.

The negotiations took uncommonly long, November 17–23 and again December 5–18, partly due to disagreements in particular between most of the IMF staff and all the other participants and partly because of the very uncertainty of the economic situation and complications involving Parex Bank. The sharp differences among these participants resulted in an unusually well written and analytical IMF staff report.

The main objectives of the program were clearly stated: "to arrest the immediate liquidity crisis and to ensure long-term external stability, while maintaining the exchange rate peg." This was to be done through measures to stabilize the financial sector and substantial fiscal policy tightening combined with structural reforms and income policies to improve competitiveness.[47] Until the end of 2008, Latvia's public finances appeared to be in good shape. The immediate reason for Latvia having to call in the IMF was the collapse of Parex Bank, and the broader concern was the country's liquidity crisis. In addition, the country needed to become more competitive. Either prices had to be brought down or production rendered more efficient. The financial crisis would undermine government finances. Five big issues dominated the negotiations: exchange rate policy, Parex Bank, economic outlook, fiscal adjustment, and the mobilization of international financing.

First, the Latvian authorities stated in no uncertain terms that the fixed exchange rate was not an issue for discussion. The IMF put it: "A change in the peg is strongly opposed by the Latvian authorities and by the EU institutions, and thus would undermine program ownership." It went further: "Any change in regime would cause significant economic, social and political disruption." The IMF accepted the Latvian position: "The program's aim is to meet the Maastricht criteria to facilitate adoption of the euro." The internal IMF discussion about devaluation continued in the staff report. The supporters of Latvia's peg included a box with 13 cases in nine countries from the last three decades of "important real exchange depreciation under currency pegs." The opponents of the peg included a final caveat: "Risks to the program are nevertheless considerable."[48]

Second, the most difficult issue was rather technical: What could and should be done with Parex Bank? The IMF staff report stated: "The authorities' first priority is to arrest the deteriorating condition in Parex Bank, as the rest of the banking system so far has been able to meet increased demands for liquidity." A second and decisive step taken on December 5 was a precondition of the IMF program: The government raised its share of Parex Bank from 51 to 85 percent of the shares and appointed new professional management to run the bank. Parex Bank had €975 million in syndicated loans, which could fall due in the first half of 2009, amounting to 4.6 percent of GDP. Another concern was that the former owners would tap the bank for money. Therefore, it was necessary to "ringfence" Parex Bank. The IMF estimated that the total fiscal costs for bank restructuring could be 15 to 20 percent of GDP through 2010.[49]

Third, economic forecasts were all a big unknown. At the time, the global economy seemed to have entered a sinkhole and nobody could predict how deep the economy would fall, but a government budget or an IMF program always needs forecasts regardless of how little basis they may have. The IMF and the Latvian government made similar predictions, but they were regularly revised downward, and the prognosis in the IMF program was way off the actual outcome. These numbers show how great the uncertainty was and how impossible it is to accurately forecast in the midst of a severe financial crisis.

While the IMF foresaw in December 2008 a 5 percent slump in 2009 GDP, the actual fall was 18 percent, as the recession was far greater than anticipated. Correspondingly, the predicted current account deficit of 7.3 percent of GDP in 2009 swung around to become a surplus of 8.6 percent of GDP. Similarly, average inflation predicted to be 5.9 percent in 2009 stopped at 3.3 percent and fell into minor deflation in 2010 (table 3.1). These numbers show a scared population that more than tightened its belt. As a result, GDP fell much more than expected, whereas the current account deficit was eliminated in no time.

Table 3.1   IMF forecasts and outcomes, 2008–10

	2008		2009		2010	
Measure	Forecast	Outcome	Forecast	Outcome	Forecast	Outcome
GDP growth (percent)	–2.0	–3.6	–5.0	–18.4	–3.0	–0.2
Inflation (percent; period average)	15.5	15.3	5.9	3.3	2.2	–1.2
Current account balance (percent of GDP)	–14.8	–13.0	–7.3	8.6	–5.5	3.6

Sources: International Monetary Fund, Republic of Latvia, "Request for Stand-By Arrangement," December 19, 2008, 1, www.imf.org (accessed on November 15, 2010); International Monetary Fund, *World Economic Outlook* database; Central Statistical Bureau of Latvia, www.csb.gov.lv (accessed on March 11, 2011).

Prices developed close to ideal, eliminating inflation but not turning into a deflationary cycle.

Fourth, major fiscal adjustments were required, but given the strong and broad Latvian commitment to the peg this was not as controversial as might be assumed. One of the first and important preconditions of the "It's Mostly Fiscal" IMF was that Latvia address its budget deficit. The parliament had passed a budget in November 2008 aiming at a budget deficit of 1 percent of GDP in 2009, but its assumptions were overoptimistic, and one month later the IMF assessed the likely budget deficit in 2009 at 12 percent of GDP, as growth forecasts fell and tax revenues, as is usual, contracted more than output.

The IMF demanded a reduction of the budget deficit by 7.1 percent of GDP, allowing for a budget deficit of 4.9 percent of GDP in 2009. Roughly two-thirds of the fiscal consolidation, or 4.6 percent of GDP, was supposed to come from cuts in public expenditure and one-third or 2.5 percent of GDP from increased taxation.

The cuts in public expenditures were enormous: a real cut of 25 percent of most current spending. All public wages were to be slashed by 25 percent in nominal terms. In addition, on December 10, the government signed a protocol with local governments compelling them to undertake the same nominal wage cuts as the central administration.[50] The focus lay on comprehensive reforms of the state and local administration, the education system, and civil service, which had been prepared for years. Yet, both the Latvian government and the IMF were anxious to maintain social expenditures. Pensions were frozen in nominal terms in 2009, and social spending was supposed to increase from 21 to 25 percent of the budget.

The Latvian government opposed abandonment of the flat income tax and the low corporate profit taxes, but it accepted with regret an increase in the value-added tax (VAT) from 18 to 21 percent, and various excise taxes were also hiked. As a result, state revenues worth about 4 percent of GDP were to be shifted from direct to indirect taxes, with the intention of enhancing economic efficiency. The IMF also favored broader capital gains taxes and real estate taxes, but nothing was decided in December 2008.

Finally, substantial financing would be required for Latvia's stabilization. How much financing would be necessary, and who could mobilize it? The IMF assessed Latvia's gross external financing requirements at close to €7.5 billion through early 2011, that is, 37 percent of Latvia's actual 2008 GDP—an unprecedented amount.[51]

International capital flows were also difficult to predict. For example, one important source of international financing was capital injections by foreign shareholders in their Latvian bank subsidiaries, which the IMF estimated would amount to as much as 9.7 percent of GDP in 2009–10 or €2.0 billion. Much depended on whether these capital injections would be provided or not.

Traditionally, the IMF had limited its lending to three times the quota a country held with the Fund. However, the IMF had already participated in the exceptionally large stabilization programs notably for South Korea and Turkey, so the ice was already broken. After Hungary had got 12 times its quota, Latvia could hardly be given less. Yet, non-European IMF members were not prepared to accept more, so Latvia obtained an IMF commitment of credits of €1.7 billion, which was only 22 percent of the financing cap of €7.5 billion.

Usually, the World Bank had also made substantial contributions to IMF financing, but during the European financial crisis the Bank decided to limit its contribution mostly to social safety networks to the tune of €400 million. The EBRD contributed €100 million. In effect, this financing was for recapitalization of Parex Bank.

The European Commission had played a pioneering role in the stabilization program for Hungary in October 2008. To the IMF's commitment of €12.3 billion, the Commission added a substantial €6.5 billion. It was drawn from the European Stabilization Fund, a balance-of-payments support facility of €12 billion that had been set up in the early 1990s to support countries in crisis in Southern Europe. The fund was meant for EU countries outside the euro area. On December 2, 2008, the European Council doubled the fund to €25 billion, so the European Union had ample funds to support Latvia.[52]

Latvia benefited from the Hungarian precedent and the reinforced EU funding. In addition, it enjoyed solid support from its Baltic and Nordic neighbors, who formed one region on the IMF board and had cut their teeth on the Icelandic crisis. Because of all these positive forces, Latvia managed to get a commitment of credits of no less than €3.1 billion from the European Commission, almost twice as much as from the IMF, and it was heavily front-loaded. No less than €2.2 billion was supposed to be disbursed over the next six months.

The total from these international organizations amounted to €5.3 billion, which still left a substantial financing gap of €2.2 billion. As the situation became clear, Swedish Minister of Finance Anders Borg called the closest friends of

Table 3.2 International financial support: Commitments and disbursements, 2008–11 (millions of euros)

Lender	Disbursements			Commitments	Total
	2008	2009	2010	2011	
European Union	—	2,200	700	200	3,100
International Monetary Fund	591	194	301	631	1,717
World Bank	—	200	100	100	400
European Bank for Reconstruction and Development	—	80	—	—	80
Nordics (Denmark, Estonia, Finland, Norway, and Sweden)	—	—	—	1,900	1,900
Poland	—	—	—	100	100
Czech Republic	—	—	—	200	200
Total	591	2,674	1,101	3,131	7,497

Source: European Commission, "Latvia: European Union Balance of Payments Assistance," EC Staff Report from the 3rd Review Mission to Riga, June 18, 2010.

Latvia to an emergency meeting at Arlanda airport in Stockholm on December 10. In a kind of auction, Borg allotted the remaining financing gap to Latvia's friends.[53] Sweden, Denmark, Norway, and Finland together committed to total credits of €1.8 billion. Impressively, three new EU members outside of the euro area made their own commitments: the Czech Republic, €200 million, Poland, €100 million, and even small Estonia, €100 million. The whole financing gap was then covered, and the IMF agreement could be concluded (table 3.2).

This bilateral funding was always perceived as a backstop. It required special parliamentary decisions in each country, which were forthcoming without problem. However, unlike the frontloaded IMF and EU funding, it was backloaded and not supposed to be disbursed until 2010 or 2011. Moreover, while the multilateral credits would cost 3 to 3.5 percent a year in interest, the bilateral funds would cost about 6 percent a year. Therefore, the Latvian government saw the bilateral funds as a reserve that it would hopefully not need, and it did not. Yet, these commitments were critical for the approval of the IMF agreement.

A peculiarity in the Latvian stabilization efforts was that the Swedish Riksbank and the Danish central bank opened a swap line of €500 million to bridge the IMF stand-by loan,[54] showing the great commitment of the Nordic countries to Latvia's stabilization. In 2007, the US Federal Reserve started offering large swap lines to the world's foremost central banks—ECB, Bank of Japan, Bank of England, and Swiss National Bank—and then extended them to nearly every advanced economy. In October 2008, the US Federal Reserve provided four emerging economies with large credit swaps: Brazil, Mexico, Singapore, and South Korea each received $30 billion.[55] This was not the

Federal Reserve's duty, but it did so because of its sense of responsibility for global financial stability.

The ECB did not have any obligation to issue swap credit lines either, but in stark contrast to the US Federal Reserve, it was indifferent to liquidity scarcity in surrounding economies, even non-euro area EU countries. The ECB offered two euro swap lines, to the Swedish Riksbank and the Danish National Bank, but it did so late. Hungary and Poland were offered repo loans, which were of no significance as they required liquid euro assets as collateral. Instead, Poland had to go to the IMF for a Flexible Credit Line, which fulfilled the same function as a swap line. If the ECB had acted as the US Federal Reserve, it would have offered swap lines to all solvent non-euro area EU countries, but it did not. Neither before, during, nor after the crisis did the ECB lift a finger for Latvia, although it is one of the shareholders of the ECB. As Adam S. Posen has argued: "A successful regional currency role for the euro would entail fulfilling responsibilities toward countries in the region that have adopted the euro as a monetary anchor or whose financial systems are partially euroized."[56] If the ECB had provided swap lines to the Baltic states, Poland, and the Czech Republic, by accepting government bonds denominated in local currencies of non-euro area EU countries as collateral, as Zsolt Darvas and Jean Pisani-Ferry advocated,[57] the output collapse in the Baltic region would in all probability have been contained.

On December 23, 2008, the IMF Executive Board speedily approved a $2.35 billion 27-month Stand-By Arrangement for Latvia and disbursed a first installment of €586 million or $860 million. The European Union also fulfilled its commitments from December but at a somewhat more leisurely pace. On January 20, 2009, the European Council decided to make up to €3.1 billion available to Latvia as medium-term financial assistance with a maximum maturity of seven years, demanding a long list of structural reforms. On February 25, it disbursed its first installment of €1 billion, securing three months of international reserves for Latvia.

Notes

1. The classical treatment is Charles P. Kindleberger and Robert Aliber, *Manias, Panics, and Crashes*, 5th ed. (Hoboken, NJ: Wiley, 2005). A recent empirical overview is Carmen M. Reinhart and Kenneth S. Rogoff, *This Time Is Different: Eight Centuries of Financial Folly* (Princeton: Princeton University Press, 2009).

2. Alexandru Rusu, *Latvia* (report, Civil Society Against Corruption, September 2010), www.againstcorruption.eu (accessed on April 6, 2011).

3. The Cabinet of Ministers of the Republic of Latvia, "Transcript of the Meeting of Prime Minister of the Republic of Latvia Valdis Dombrovskis with the Representatives of the International Mass Media on Monday, March 23, 2009," State Chancellery, March 27, 2009, www.mk.gov.lv (accessed on December 7, 2010); Economist Intelligence Unit, "Latvia Politics: Godmanis's New/Old Government" (Country Briefing, January 28, 2008), www.eiu.com (accessed on April 8, 2011).

4. Lars Christensen, "Unwinding New Europe Imbalances—How Bad Will It Be?" Danske Bank, July 2008, www.danskebank.dk.

5. This notion was coined by Rudiger Dornbusch, Ilan Goldfajn, and Rodrigo O. Valdés, "Currency Crises and Collapses," *Brookings Papers on Economic Activity* 26 (1995): 219-93; and elaborated upon by Guillermo A. Calvo, "Capital Flows and Capital-Market Crises: The Simple Economics of Sudden Stops," *Journal of Applied Economics* 1, no. 1 (1998): 35-54.

6. International Monetary Fund, Republic of Latvia, "Request for Stand-By Arrangement," December 19, 2008, p. 8, www.imf.org (accessed on November 15, 2010).

7. Jean Pisani-Ferry and Adam S. Posen, eds. *The Euro at Ten: The Next Global Currency* (Washington: Peterson Institute for International Economics, 2009, 5).

8. European Investment Bank, "EU Funds Co-Financing 2007-13 (LV)," www.eib.org; Ministry of Finance of the Republic of Latvia, "Latvia ensures 500 million euro financing," news release, October 23, 2008, www.fm.gov.lv (accessed on January 27, 2011).

9. Aaron Eglitis, "Latvia May Return to Eurobond Market Next Year, Finance Chief Vilks Says," Bloomberg, December 17, 2010.

10. LETA, "Latvijā sākas mediķu streiks" ["Latvian Doctors Begin Protest"], October 30, 2008.

11. DELFI, "TP valde nevērtē Slaktera došanos atvaļinājumā budžeta izskatīšanas laikā" ["People's Party Council Will Not Evaluate Slaketeris Going on Holiday on the Eve of Budget Adoption"], October 28, 2008, www.delfi.lv.

12. Eurostat, "Industrial production up by 1.1% in euro area," news release, October 14, 2008.

13. Eurostat, "Volume of retail trade up by 0.3% in euro area," news release, October 3, 2008.

14. Eurostat, "Euro area unemployment up to 7.7%," news release, November 28, 2008.

15. LETA, "Koalitsiya uverena v sposobnosti rabotat' vmeste" ["The Coalition Is Sure of Its Ability to Work Together"], November 6, 2008; DELFI, "Opozīcija kritizē valdības sagatavotos grozījumus kapitālsabiedrību likumā; demisiju nepieprasa" ["Opposition Criticizes the Amendments Proposed by the Government...Does Not Demand Resignation of Godmanis"], November 13, 2008, www.delfi.lv.

16. Artem Yefimov, "Pravitel'stvo sokratit raskhody na armiyu" ["The Government Will Reduce Military Spending"], *Biznes & Baltiya*, November 3, 2008.

17. DELFI, "Ministr: budushchiy god budet neprognoziruemym" ["Minister: The Next Year Will Be Unpredictable"], November 20, 2008, www.delfi.lv.

18. LETA, "Politiki obeshchayut ne speshit' s byudzhetom-2009" ["Politicians Promise Not to Rush with the 2009 Budget"], October 17, 2008.

19. DELFI, "Seim utverdil byudzhet na 2009 god" ["The Seim Has Approved the Budget for 2009"], November 14, 2008, www.delfi.lv.

20. LETA, "Prem'er: 'islandskiy stsenariy' v Latvii nevozmozhen" ["Prime Minister: The Icelandic Scenario Is Impossible in Latvia"], October 28, 2008.

21. DELFI, "Laikraksts: Godmaņa valdība kritīs pavasarī" ["Newspaper: The Godmanis Government Will Fall in the Spring"], October 17, 2008, www.delfi.lv.

22. LETA, "Šķēle kritizē valsts budžetu un aicina negraut pensiju sistēmu" ["Šķēle Criticizes the Government's Budget and Warns About Breaking Pension System"], October 18, 2008.

23. DELFI, "Shkele: sleduyushchiy god budet kriticheskim" ["Shkele: The Next Year Will Be Crucial"], October 30, 2008, www.delfi.lv.

24. DELFI, "Zatlers gatavs iespējai, ka Godmaņa valdība var krist" ["Zatlers is Prepared for the Possibility that the Godmanis Government May Collapse"], October 21, 2008, www.delfi.lv.

25. DELFI, "Zatlers: narod podderzhal by rospusk Seima" ["Zatlers; The People Would Support Dissolution of Seima"] October 27, 2008, www.delfi.lv.

26. LETA, "Zatlers: TP ir atbildīga, ka Latvija nav pienācīgi sagatavojusies finanšu krīzei" ["Zatlers: People's Party Responds that Latvia Is Unprepared for the Financial Crisis"], November 20, 2008.

27. DELFI, "Zatlers: pravitel'stvo Godmanisa otstoyalo tsennosti" ["Zalters: The Government of Godmanis Has Insisted upon Values"], December 19, 2008, www.delfi.lv.

28. Central Statistical Bureau of Latvia, "Main commodities and partners in January-September 2008," November 20, 2008, www.csb.gov.lv (accessed on January 27, 2010).

29. Pavel Kirillov, "Zhiteli Latvii aktivno skupayut evro" ["Residents of Latvia Are Actively Purchasing Euros"], Chas, November 19, 2008.

30. Susan Schadler, "Are Large External Imbalances in Central Europe Sustainable," in Challenges of Globalization: Imbalances and Growth, ed. Anders Åslund and Marek Dabrowski (Washington: Peterson Institute for International Economics, 2008, 38).

31. International Monetary Fund, Republic of Latvia, "Request for Stand-By Arrangement," 8.

32. DELFI, "Godmanis: esli kredit ne budet poluchen, u byudzheta mogut vozniknut' problemy" ["Godmanis: If Credit Is Not Received, Problems May Arise with the Budget"], December 4, 2010, www.delfi.lv.

33. "V Latvii kazhdyi pyatyi—bezrabotnyi" ["In Latvia One in Five Will Be Unemployed"], Biznes & Baltiya, December 10, 2008.

34. Robert Anderson, "Latvia's IMF Talks Stall over Bank Deal," Financial Times, December 2, 2008; Robert Anderson, "Latvia Nationalises Parex Bank As Depositors Withdraw Faith," Financial Times, December 4, 2008; personal observation of billboards in Stockholm.

35. Toomas Hõbemägi, "Parex Bank sues former owners Kargins, Krasovickis," Baltic Business News, August 2, 2010, www.balticbusinessnews.com (accessed on April 12, 2011); Nina Kolyako, "Parex bank starts proceedings against Kargins and Krasovickis," Baltic Course, July 31, 2010, www.baltic-course.com/eng (accessed on April 12, 2011).

36. Kira Savchenko, "Prem'er oglasil tainyi plan" ["The Prime Minister Announced the Covert Plan"], Biznes & Baltiya, December 5, 2008. It is unclear to whom Slakteris referred.

37. "Programma spaseniya ekonomiki—zasekrechena" ["Program for Rescuing the Economy—Classified"], Biznes & Baltiya, December 2, 2008.

38. LETA, "Godmanis nepiekāpjas sociālajiem partneriem nodokļu politikas jautājumā" ["Godmanis Does Not Yield to Partners on Issues Relating to Taxation"], December 10, 2008.

39. Jānis Urbanovičs, "Kas vainīgs un ko darīt?" ["Who Is to Blame and What Should Be Done?"], DELFI, December 10, 2008, www.delfi.lv.

40. DELFI, "Oppozitsiya raskritikovala stabplan" ["The Opposition Criticized the Stabilization Plan"] December 11, 2008, www.delfi.lv; "TsS: Eto samy plokhoi byudzhet s 1991 goda" ["Harmony Center: This Is the Worst Budget Since 1991"], November 15, 2008.

41. Aigars Štokenbergs, "Cik naudas vajag Latvijai?" ["How Much Money Does Latvia Need?"], DELFI, December 10, 2008, www.delfi.lv.

42. DELFI, "Dlya uvol'neniya Slakterisa ne khvatilo golosov" ["Not Enough Votes Were Obtained to Fire Slakteris"], December 12, 2008, www.delfi.lv.

43. Urbanovičs, "Kas vainīgs un ko darīt?" ["Who Is to Blame and What Should Be Done?"]

44. Ministry of Finance, "Latvia's Economic Stabilization and Growth Revival Program," December 12, 2008, www.mk.gov.lv (accessed on December 7, 2010).

45. International Monetary Fund, Republic of Latvia, "Request for Stand-By Arrangement," 1.

46. Ibid.

47. Ibid.

48. Ibid., 9–10, 25, 28.

49. Ibid., 6–7, 12, 17.

50. Ibid., 14–17, 30.

51. Ibid., 18–20.

52. Anders Åslund, *The Last Shall Be the First: The East European Financial Crisis, 2008–10* (Washington: Peterson Institute for International Economics, 2010, 78). On May 18, 2009, this fund was doubled again to €50 billion.

53. "Operation Baltikum," *Affärsvärlden*, February 20, 2009.

54. International Monetary Fund, Republic of Latvia, "Request for Stand-By Arrangement," 20. Robert Anderson, "Latvia to Receive Central Bank Help," *Financial Times*, December 17, 2008.

55. Maurice Obstfeld, Jay C. Shambaugh, and Alan M. Taylor, "Financial Instability, Reserves, and Central Bank Swap Lines in the Panic of 2008," NBER Working Paper 14826 (Cambridge, MA: National Bureau of Economic Research, 2008).

56. Adam S. Posen, "Geopolitical Limits of the Euro's Global Role," in *The Euro at Ten: The Next Global Currency*, eds. Jean Pisani-Ferry and Adam Posen (Washington: Peterson Institute for International Economics, 2009, 93).

57. Zsolt Darvas and Jean Pisani-Ferry, "Eastern European Currencies Need Help Now," *Wall Street Journal*, March 12, 2009.

4

To Devalue or Not to Devalue

The Latvian financial stabilization program ignited a fiery policy debate about exchange rate devaluation. This debate took place in many places: Latvia, the International Monetary Fund (IMF), the European Commission, European capitals, and among international economists. It was most intense in December 2008–January 2009 and again in June 2009.

Both opponents and proponents of devaluation agreed that Latvia suffered from massive financial overheating. It was reflected in too large credit expansion, too high inflation, too fast wage rises, and especially rapid hikes in real estate prices. All these had resulted in excessive current account deficits and considerable private foreign debt. But the two camps were polarized over what had to be done about the financial crisis that followed the sudden stop in capital inflows. Most Balts opposed devaluation, and their closest European allies concurred, while most American economists favored devaluation. It was not a matter of political views but rather of differing insights and economic outlook.

Arguments for a Fixed Exchange Rate

In Latvia the question whether to devalue was barely an issue.[1] A broad consensus held that Latvia must not devalue, and the topic was rather how Latvia could avoid devaluation. The same was true in Estonia, Lithuania, and Bulgaria, the three other EU countries with currency boards. The fixed exchange rate was a sacred cow. The Latvian government recognized the mistakes of the previous economic policy and hammered out a clear line of arguments, around which a broad consensus evolved.[2]

First, the Baltic countries' experience with firm pegs had been excellent. In the early 1990s, these nominal anchors contributed to budgetary and macroeconomic discipline, facilitating swift financial stabilization and market economic transformation. In the ensuing years, the peg helped to improve the business climate and attract foreign direct investment. During the Russian financial crisis of 1998, Latvia steadfastly refused to devalue, which contributed to its unprecedented boom in the 2000s. The peg had steered the country onto the right track in both macroeconomic and microeconomic policies. The Latvian population was acutely aware of this success and wanted to maintain the pegged exchange rate at almost any price. As one of us (Anders Åslund) wrote in December 2008: "the Latvian population seems politically committed to the fixed exchange rate and it seems prepared to take a freeze of incomes and public expenditures, and if necessary even cuts. Therefore, devaluation could lead to undesirable and unwarranted political convulsions."[3]

Second, in 1997–98, most East Asian crisis countries had devalued, breaking their banking systems at great social cost and forcing large private bank losses upon their governments. If the banks had not collapsed, the cost of the financial crisis would have been much less. The Latvians abhorred the Russian financial crash of 1998 as an example of what not to do. That disorderly devaluation had reduced the value of the ruble by over 75 percent and bankrupted half the banks. Also the devaluations of Finland and Sweden in the early 1990s deterred them. Bank of Latvia Governor Ilmars Rimšēvičs noted: In "Finland, the decline in GDP continued for two years after the devaluation."[4] The Latvian government was compelled to recapitalize Parex Bank, but without devaluation it had hope of avoiding costs from other bank crashes.

Third, devaluations in crisis tend to overshoot, and the thinner the market the greater the risk. After markets have lost confidence, it is difficult to reestablish credibility, and meanwhile everything is falling—the exchange rate, real estate prices, stock prices, and bond prices. All lat markets were extremely thin, as the lat was used in so few transactions, so devaluation would have to be large—perhaps 50 percent, for no good economic reasons. Such an overshooting would have been disruptive and could have incited devastating financial panic.

Fourth, uncontrolled depreciation would have effectively bankrupted Latvia, as the gross foreign debt of 135 percent of GDP at the end of 2008 would have doubled with a devaluation of, say, 50 percent. As the IMF put it: "Devaluation would create large balance sheet effects, with a risk of negative feedback loops. Some 70 percent of bank deposits and nearly 90 percent of loans are foreign currency denominated. ...any change in the nominal exchange rate would lead to an immediate deterioration in private sector net worth."[5] Therefore, devaluation might not have significantly reduced the need for external financing.

Fifth, the Latvians realized that in their small and open economy the pass-through of imported inflation would be great and any competitiveness gain through devaluation brief. Energy prices would increase immediately at home after devaluation, as would many component prices. Latvia would not have benefited from any lasting price reduction but been condemned to high inflation.

Sixth, Latvia needed more structural reforms, and the maintenance of the peg could help the government accomplish that. During the boom years since 2004, few reforms had been attempted and a backlog of desired reforms had built up, particularly in the public sector. A large fiscal adjustment would prompt such reforms.

Seventh, devaluation would substantially redistribute wealth from most of society to a few big exporters. Lats were mainly used for paying wages and taxes as well as in domestic trade. Therefore, devaluation would in all likelihood reduce wages far more in euro terms than direct wage cuts would, and in this highly euroized economy people measured their incomes in euro.

Eighth, Latvia was committed to early adoption of the euro, which was its natural exit from the fixed exchange rate. It entered the European Exchange Rate Mechanism (ERM II) in 2005—which is a passage intended to last two to three years before aspiring euro adopters are allowed to adopt the euro. However, inflation had taken off in 2004 and persistently exceeded the Maastricht inflation ceiling: Average inflation rate one year prior to entry in the Economic and Monetary Union (EMU) must not exceed the average of the lowest three inflation rates of the EU member countries by more than 1.5 percentage points. If Latvia had devalued, inflation would have shot up again and it would have been close to impossible for Latvia to join the EMU. If Latvia insisted on its peg, on the contrary, prices would fall and Latvia would be able to enter as soon as its budget deficit had been contained under the Maastricht fiscal criterion of 3 percent of GDP.

Ninth, devaluation would have serious international repercussions. Estonia and Lithuania were in similar but not quite as severe financial crises. If Latvia had devalued, they would probably have been forced to do so as well, which would have devastated their bank systems, and their demand, which is important for Latvia's exports, would have plummeted. If multiple banks collapsed in all three Baltic countries, the two Swedish banks Swedbank and SEB would be in serious trouble. During the onset of the crisis in the fall of 2008, the exchange rate of the floating currencies in the region—notably, the Swedish krona and the Polish zloty—fell sharply, and they were again influenced by the devaluation scare in early June 2009. This argument carried a lot of weight with the EU and neighboring countries and with some in the IMF.

Tenth, the last thing the global economy needed was another concentrated shock in the midst of the Great Recession, as Mary Stokes elaborated:

> Devaluation would lead to a wave of defaults occurring in a concentrated period. Internal deflation would also result in defaults, but they would likely be spread over a more protracted period... [which] would result in less financial instability in Latvia and beyond....

> The departure of [the Swedish] banks from the Baltics would be a massive blow to financial stability and consequently, it would impede economic recovery in the Baltics, as these Swedish banks make up the bulk of these countries' financial systems... Arguably, if the defaults occur over a more extended period of time...these Swedish banks might better absorb losses and weather the storm.[6]

Finally, Latvia could attract uniquely large international rescue funds in relation to the size of its economy. With a public debt of only 9 percent of GDP at the end of 2007, the country was eminently creditworthy at the onset of the crisis. Its market reforms and governance were exemplary. A strong argument could be made that Latvia's problems were of a temporary, cyclical nature, not involving long-term solidity. As a member of the European Union and a peer of the Nordic countries, Latvia could count on substantial financial support.

It was widely accepted that Latvia had priced itself out of the market, but given the fast recovery of exports and the comparatively limited rise in real effective exchange rate (figure 2.7), this was hardly true. Nor did Latvia suffer from any terms-of-trade shock, as was the case with commodity exporters Ukraine and Russia, for whom devaluation made perfect sense.

The main shock to Latvia was the sudden stop with near complete freezing of international finance. Considering that the European Central Bank (ECB) did not offer any liquidity, the dearth of credit was severe until market interest rates normalized by March 2010 (figure 5.6).

The responsibility for exchange rate policy varies between countries. It can rest with the government or the central bank or be their joint responsibility. In Latvia, the central bank, the Bank of Latvia, is fully in charge and enjoys great independence. Rimšēvičs has persistently expressed his strong commitment to the fixed exchange rate of the lat, with statements like: "The Bank of Latvia has repeatedly underlined that devaluation of the lat would not be a cure for the national economy but poison."[7]

In the international debate, unilateral euroization was mentioned as a possibility. Kosovo and Montenegro, which were not even members of the European Union, had unilaterally adopted the euro as their national currency, and it helped them maintain financial stability during the crisis. For Latvia, however, this option was legally precluded. The European Union and the ECB were categorically opposed to unilateral euroization, and as a member of the European Union and coowner of the ECB, Latvia neither could nor desired to go against their view. It wanted to adopt the euro as a full-fledged member of the euro area and its governing bodies.

The natural conclusion of these arguments was to pursue "internal devaluation" rather than external devaluation, which meant carrying out structural reforms to raise productivity, cutting the least beneficial parts of the public sector and enhancing its efficiency, and reducing wages and pensions as necessary. The questions that remained were the types of measures and their intensity, while the alternative—devaluation—was precluded.

Arguments for Devaluation

A varied group of international economists, most with minimal knowledge about the Baltic states, argued that the Baltics had to devalue. This was the overwhelming view in the public debate, in English at least, for Latvia. The most thoughtful proponent of devaluation in Latvia, Edward Hugh, noted: "There are relatively few people, at least in the English language, who are willing to stick their neck out and try to justify what, in my humble opinion, is virtually the unjustifiable, and the implicit consensus among thinking economists would seem to be that this is a bad idea. The decision does, however, have its advocates, and Anders Aslund of the Peterson Institute has been bold enough to have a try...."[8]

The dominant public argument soon became that Latvia was the new Argentina, referring to the disorderly devaluation and ensuing horrendous financial meltdown there in 2001. An early article on these lines is worth quoting at some length to show the quality of that discussion:

> The Baltics are looking a lot like Argentina was before it collapsed at the beginning of the decade: fixed exchange rate, large current account deficit, significant foreign bank lending, overheating economy turning to bust. This combination is a toxic mix that will certainly end in the disaster it did for Argentina....
>
> The Baltics have a lot of hot money invested in their economies as much of the lending growth came on the back of foreign financial investment. When distress hits, one should expect a giant sucking noise from foreigners repatriating funds. This will leave the Baltics subject to credit deflation just as the economy is entering recession.
>
> When one adds the slow economy and the high inflation to a fixed exchange rate and high current account deficits it says: the Baltics do not have the appropriate fiscal and monetary policy for a fixed exchange rate.
>
> One of two things must give: the exchange rate peg or the economy. In Argentina, it was both.[9]

In December 2008, Nobel laureate and *New York Times* columnist Paul Krugman picked up this theme, and it became the conventional wisdom at least in America: "The most acute problems are on Europe's periphery, where many smaller economies are experiencing crisis strongly reminiscent of past crises in Latin America and Asia: Latvia is the new Argentina."[10] Professor Krugman does not appear to have developed his argument much but concluded: "A nominal devaluation and a real depreciation achieved through deflation should have exactly the same effect on debt service (unless some of the debt is in lats rather than euros, in which case devaluation would do less damage.)"[11]

More serious arguments were presented by Edward Hugh, Nouriel Roubini, and Simon Johnson.[12] Their criticism was directed against the IMF and its Stand-By Arrangement with Latvia of December 19, which presupposed the maintenance of the fixed exchange rate.

A first argument was that Latvia's competitiveness had fallen too sharply, as reflected in the real effective exchange rate and in the large current account deficit. Devaluation was seen as the only plausible means of adjustment.

Second, many argued that internal devaluation was impossible because of issues of political economy: "The kind of internal deflation process the Latvian government has just accepted is normally very difficult to implement, which is why economists tend to favor the devaluation approach."[13] But Hugh took this argument further to an asserted impossibility:

> Indeed I am almost certain that the attempt to sustain [the fixed exchange rate] will fail (and that we will see some kind of rerun of Argentina 2000—in all three Baltic countries and Bulgaria) and really the sooner the population become aware of this the better... what we witnessed in Argentina in 2000 was basically a process of growing battle fatigue and war weariness, as the population were asked to make one sacrifice after another in support of a policy which couldn't work, and only lasted as long as it could. The end product is that when the peg finally breaks the local population will be severely disillusioned, and the politicians will totally lack credibility, which is a sure recipe for chaos, as we saw in Argentina in 2001.

A third argument was that Latvia needed demand stimulus. Western economists who were caught up in the US economic debate about Keynesian stimulus through loose monetary and fiscal policy were focused on possible sources of demand. Hugh argued: "Basically I feel the biggest condemnation which can be made of the package which has been announced is that it doesn't seem to contain one single policy for stimulating the economy, and stimulation and a return to growth is what Latvia badly needs by now."[14] Similarly, Roubini contended: "Draconian cuts in public spending will be required if Latvia is to improve the current account. But this is becoming politically unsustainable. And while fiscal consolidation is needed—as Argentina found in 2000–01—it will make the recession more severe in the short run. So it is a self-defeating strategy as long as the currency remains overvalued."[15]

Fourth, the proponents of devaluation feared that Latvia otherwise would enter a deflationary cycle with GDP and prices chasing each other ever lower. In Hugh's words: "Thus we could see a very large drop in nominal GDP in 2009 and 2010. If realized this would be a very difficult situation to handle, and I doubt the people currently taking policy decisions in Latvia are fully aware of the implications (although the IMF economists should know better). In particular the deflationary debt dynamics would be very hard to control, and again, especially without independent monetary policy."[16] A leftwing proponent of devaluation, Michael Hudson, envisioned a deflationary cycle: "The problem is that austerity prompts strikes and slowdowns, which, in turn, shrink the domestic market, investment and tax receipts."[17]

Fifth, the proponents of devaluation harbored the view that inflation could be controlled through independent monetary policy.

Sixth, they did not care about the proliferation of the crisis to the other currency board countries, Estonia, Lithuania, and possibly Bulgaria, as they considered devaluation inevitable. They presumed mass defaults would occur in any case and argued that Latvia should not be forced to bear the costs of

Swedish bank mortgages but default on them.[18] Two related arguments—once again about Argentina—were that a government should not nationalize private losses or take public loans to cover such private losses.

Seventh, some thought that Latvia should not be helped, for the sake of fairness. Devesh Kapur and Arvind Subramanian complained about the IMF being a "Euro-Atlantic Monetary Fund."[19] Kenneth Rogoff, former IMF chief economist, stated that the IMF made the wrong decision when it allowed Latvia to keep its currency peg. In a normal situation, Latvia would already have devalued the lat and defaulted on its debt.[20]

Eighth, an odd presumption was that Latvia had nothing to export. Hugh was comparatively polite: "Perhaps the best indication of the severity of the problem is the way that people almost laugh at the suggestion that Latvia must now live from exports (exports, what exports?, they say)."[21] Others put it simply: "But Latvia doesn't produce much to export."[22] Well, small countries do not. What matters is whether they can balance their current account. Hudson attacked the very building of capitalism in these countries: "The problem is that Latvia, like other post-Soviet economies, has scant domestic output to export. Industry throughout the former Soviet Union was torn up and scrapped in the 1990s."[23]

Finally, leftwing rhetoric and capitalist imperialist conspiracy theories entered the stage: "In Latvia, the neo-liberal insanity continues. The EU and IMF have told the government to borrow foreign currency to stabilize the exchange rate to help real estate debtors pay their foreign-currency mortgages taken out from Swedish and other banks to fuel its property bubble, raise taxes, and sharply cut back public spending on education, health care and other basic needs to 'absorb' income."[24] Some leftwingers attacked Latvia's popular flat personal income tax: "Latvia is an extreme example: its flat taxes fall almost entirely on employment...."[25] In particular, the Washington-based leftwing think tank Center for Economic and Policy Research (CEPR) engaged with Latvia, putting up a large number of publications on its website and other outlets in Latvia and abroad. In Latvia's October 2010 elections, the CEPR cooperated with Harmony Center.[26]

In the end, economists who favored devaluation saw it as inevitable, which meant they were right by definition. Roubini was illustrative: "Nonetheless, devaluation seems unavoidable and the IMF programme—which ruled it out—is thus inherently flawed. The IMF or the European Union could increase financial support for Latvia but, as in Argentina this would be throwing good money after bad."[27]

Roubini favored a limited, controlled devaluation to be followed by an immediate euroization: "To minimize the risk of contagion, the best strategy may be: depreciate the currency, euroise after depreciation, restructure private foreign currency liabilities without a formal 'default,' and augment the IMF plan to limit the fallout."[28] Such a policy would have made sense, if it had been politically possible, but because of ECB and EU opposition, it was not an option. As the IMF Stand-By Arrangement stated: "The EU authorities have firmly ruled out this option, given its inconsistency with the Maastricht Treaty and the precedents it would set for other potential euro area entrants."[29]

The bottom line of the proponents of devaluation was that the austerity policies required to escape the crisis would be so severe that no government could manage to carry them out. Therefore devaluation would become necessary, and its cost would be less if it happened early on.

But no devaluation occurred, proving that it was not inevitable. These discussants failed to understand Latvia's political economy, which they largely ignored or equated with that of Argentina. They were also wrong on deflation, and the current account turned around faster than anybody dared hope, but their pessimistic assessment of big GDP falls was reasonable.

Latvia's main problem was not competitiveness but excessive capital inflows, followed by their sudden stop. Internal devaluation turned out to be possible. The calls for fiscal and monetary stimulation were quite incomprehensible. As the country had suffered from massive overheating, a cooling down and economic contraction seemed both desirable and inevitable. The IMF actually assessed that output exceeded potential by no less than 9 percent in 2007, so output had to contract.[30] The business cycle had not been disinvented, and this country had to adjust after an unsustainable eight-year boom. Could any policy have prevented GDP from declining? And given the size of the imbalances, was it desirable?

The Latvians did not think they could easily control inflation, painfully aware of how small and open their economy is, and many in other small European economies thought the same. This was one of the reasons why the European Monetary System, which later became the EMU, was established, and a small open economy such as Denmark had successfully maintained a peg with the deutsche mark/euro since 1982. About half the countries in the world have pegged exchange rates, so it is standard procedure, of which surprisingly many economists seemed unaware. If bank defaults are kept low through the avoidance of devaluation, public costs of bank defaults become less.

How Latvia Differs from Argentina

It should be obvious how different Latvia is from Argentina, but judging from the frequent references to Argentina in the international debate about Latvian economic policy, we need to clarify these differences.[31]

To quote Steve Hanke: "Just what, if anything, does Latvia today have in common with Argentina in 2001?"[32] Both had fixed exchange rates and incomplete currency board systems, which contributed to overvaluation of the exchange rate because of excessive inflation and large current account deficits. They also experienced a severe financial crisis and required large IMF programs, but the similarities stop there. Argentina's calamitous devaluation was a costly failure, as it devastated the banking system and the economy. Rather than following Argentina into the abyss, Latvia could use Argentina as a warning on what not to do. Many economists have a sloppy habit of establishing "stylized facts" instead of pursuing a serious empirical analysis.

Argentina's failure was not a given. In his excellent book, *Argentina and the Fund: From Triumph to Tragedy*, Michael Mussa points out that "the tragedy in Argentina is epic not because, as in most tragedies, it was inevitable, but because it was avoidable."[33] Argentina's economy had performed very well in the 1990s.

The differences between Latvia and Argentina are many and important:

- The fundamental cause of Argentina's collapse was a large and persistent public budget deficit, while Latvia had a nearly balanced budget before the crisis.
- Argentina had a large public debt of about 50 percent of GDP, whereas Latvia's was 9 percent of GDP at the end of 2007.
- Latvia is a very open economy, but Argentina is rather closed.
- Latvia has a highly flexible economy and labor market allowing wage and price cuts, while Argentina had strong entrenched interests breeding inertia.
- Latvia is a member of the European Union with the other Baltic and Scandinavian countries as supportive peer countries that were prepared to offer ample financial support, while Argentina has been on its own.
- Latvia has a natural exit from its euro peg, namely the adoption of the euro, unlike Argentina.
- Argentina had a long history of economic populism, a long-lasting record of high inflation, failed reforms, and stabilization programs and a large number of external defaults, while Latvia had a stellar history of reforms and economic responsibility.
- Politics are quite easy in the small Latvian world of broad consensus and economic virtue, while Argentine politics have usually been populist and difficult.
- Latvia is a unitary state, but Argentina is a federation with complex regional interests, where states have constitutional rights to withhold their revenues from the federal government.
- Latvia is a newly reborn state anxious to preserve its independence, as it lost one-quarter of its population in World War II through death, deportation, and emigration, while Argentina faces no foreign threat worth mentioning.
- Finally, it was easy to speculate against Argentina but almost impossible to do so against Latvia. In 2000, the Argentine government was the largest emerging-market borrower on international credit markets, with more than 20 percent of the entire asset class.[34] Latvia barely had international bonds.

The only argument for an early devaluation in Latvia was that it would become necessary in any case. Meanwhile the country's debt would rise and aggravate the crisis, and IMF credits, unlike debt to private lenders, cannot be written off. Therefore a stabilization program had to be sufficiently rigorous and the government strong enough to carry out the necessary fiscal cuts and structural reforms. In Argentina, these abilities had been lacking, but that was no reason to expect Latvia to fail as well.

The IMF Verdict

The choice to devalue or not was momentous, and the quantitative effects of either alternative could not be predicted with any degree of precision. In December 2008, nobody could guess how much GDP would plummet in 2009. The IMF forecasted 5 percent, but the slump turned out to be 18 percent.

Ultimately, the issue was not that devaluation was inevitable or that internal devaluation was impossible. It was a political choice. Tony Barber wrote in the *Financial Times*:

> My view is that, like most difficult economic choices in democracies, this is in the end a political matter. If Latvians are prepared to tough it out, and if the Latvian political classes have the stomach to preside over years of horrendous deflation then they should be free to go for it.... It is clear that the only reason the Latvians think it is worth accepting this pain is because they have a burning desire to join the eurozone....
>
> What EU policymakers should really be looking at is a way to accelerate Latvia's entry into the eurozone, so that the economic pain and social strains associated with sticking to the currency peg last for as short a time as possible.[35]

Christoph Rosenberg, the IMF mission chief to Latvia during the negotiations of the Stand-By Arrangement over the six weeks before Christmas, responded to all these arguments, mainly to Edward Hugh.[36] Rosenberg came out in full support of the Latvian position, but he appears to have been the only IMF representative to have done so. His response provides a full and eloquent argument for the maintenance of the peg, making it worthwhile to quote at length. He agreed with

> much of Hugh's analysis of what has gone wrong in Latvia. The post-EU accession boom, fueled by rapid credit and wage growth, brought Chinese-style growth rates but led to an overheated economy (a point made by the IMF as early as 2005). The bubble burst in mid-2007, when foreign banks slowed their lending, and output has been decelerating ever since. The global financial crisis, by triggering the liquidity problems at Parex...dealt the final blow.
>
> The IMF-supported program addresses both the short-term liquidity problem—by providing official financing at low interest rates—and the long-term issues associated with an overvalued real exchange rate and the private sector's debt overhang. Where I disagree with Edward Hugh, Paul Krugman and others is that the latter can only be addressed by nominal devaluation. The alternative route to external balance, adjustment via factor prices, may be

drawn-out and painful. But at this point in time it corresponds more to the circumstances in Latvia than meets the eye from [the] blogosphere. Here are nine reasons why.

First and foremost, this is the Latvians' program. So even if we at the IMF were to favor a devaluation (which we aren't), a program without national ownership would be doomed to fail.... The policymakers there are keenly aware of the choice they face. Why else would the Latvian parliament, with votes from the opposition, approve a supplementary budget that entails 7 ppt fiscal adjustment, including a 25 percent wage cut for all public servants?

Secondly, a devaluation in Latvia would have severe regional contagion effects, especially given the fragile global funding environment. The spill-overs could well go beyond pressures on countries with fixed exchange rate in the Baltics and South-East Europe. For example, market confidence in foreign banks invested in the Baltics and similar countries would likely be affected, with implications for their ability to access wholesale financing.

This is why, thirdly, Latvia's preference for the peg is strongly supported by all foreign stakeholders, including the EU and its Nordic neighbors. They have put their money where their mouth is, providing three quarters of the total financial package of EUR 7.5 billion that backs the peg. In a remarkable show of solidarity, three new EU member states—the Czech Republic, Poland and Estonia—also contributed. The Swedish, Danish and Norwegian banks operating in Latvia are doing their part by publicly committing to support the liquidity and capital needs of their Baltic subsidiaries. Given the long-term bricks and mortar investments made in the region, it seems unlikely that they will cut their losses and pull out, as Japanese banks did during the Asian crisis.

Fourth, a devaluation would not significantly reduce Latvia's external financing needs. While it would shrink the current account deficit further, private sector roll-over rates might not improve because the higher external debt to GDP ratio would likely result in credit agency downgrades to junk status and trigger the immediate repayment of most syndicated loans. Once unhinged, the peg may come under speculative pressures again and even larger external financing may be needed to credibly defend it at its new level.

Fifth, and now I turn to the internal adjustment discussed by several bloggers, there are advantages to a U-shaped adjustment via factor price compression over the V-shaped recovery that is often associated with a devaluation... devaluation—depending on its size—would lead to a wave of defaults in a concentrated period of time. Latvia's banks (both domestic and foreign) and its legal system are at this point not prepared for such a shock....

Sixth,...it is questionable whether a devaluation would quickly boost exports, given the global environment and the structure of its exports. Moreover, Latvia is a very small open economy and many of its retailers operate across all three Baltic states and set uniform prices (for all three countries) in euros. The pass-through would be high and the effect on the real exchange rate small.

Seventh, Latvia has a very flexible economy, especially a quite nimble labor market. Wage cuts up to 25 percent may seem large, but let's not forget that this comes after the tripling of nominal wages during 2001–07 (doubling in real terms) and that most of it will be accomplished by cutting bonuses of up to five monthly salaries. Latvia once before went through such factor price adjustments while maintaining its peg, during the Russian crisis in 1998. While circumstances may differ now, this experience suggests that it could do so again....

Eighth, the large-scale fiscal adjustment under the program is in line with [the] experience of successful such episodes elsewhere and therefore provides some assurances that it will not undermine the currency peg.... Roughly one third of the adjustment comes from revenue measures (increases in indirect rather than direct taxes to support wage deflation) and two thirds from cutting expenditures (wages and spending on goods and services). It was important to us at the IMF and the authorities that the 2009 budget fully protects two essential expenditure categories: cofinancing of EU-supported capital projects and social spending, which is set to increase as a share of GDP compared to 2008. The program also contains institutional reforms to put the expenditure reduction on a permanent footing.

Finally, Latvia has a clear exit strategy from its currency predicament: euro adoption. The authorities are determined to meet the Maastricht criteria in 2012.[37]

However, the IMF view was not as single-minded as Rosenberg presented it. In December 2010, the official IMF Article IV Consultation with Latvia spelled out the IMF staff thinking most clearly. One alternative it considered was "exchange rate depreciation, probably through step adjustment of the peg combined with full use of the +/−15 percent margins allowed under ERMII," but this alternative would be unrealistic without much greater intervention than the IMF could offer. Therefore, the IMF staff envisioned "the prospect of credible ECB intervention if these bands were tested," which appears unrealistic given the spectacular disinterest of the ECB in the Baltic financial crisis.[38]

Another specific alternative discussed by the IMF staff was "accelerated euro introduction at a depreciated rate, although this latter option was dismissed as inconsistent with the Maastricht Treaty." Only the IMF wanted this option, rendering it unrealistic. Latvia, the European Union, and the ECB were all against it. Latvia wanted full participation in the ECB when it adopted the euro, and it wanted to play by the rules.

The IMF report makes this overall assessment:

Depreciation would have boosted exports, allowed lower interest rates, and eased the pressures on international reserves, although high pass-through could have led to rapid inflation and limited the competitiveness benefits. However, given the high share of foreign currency borrowing, depreciation would have immediately damaged household and corporate balance sheets. This could have resulted in private sector defaults, collapsing domestic demand and a deeper initial recession.... Perhaps the strongest—and hardest to quantify—argument against depreciation was the risk it would encourage speculative attacks against other European countries with pegs. Post Lehman Brothers, the outcome of this could have been quite uncertain.[39]

This seems a fair judgment and does not make depreciation seem an attractive option. The benefits were uncertain, and the risks, both domestically and internationally, were considerable. A Latvian devaluation could have been even worse than the collapse of the European Monetary System in 1992, since the international situation was so much more unstable and uncertain.

Notes

1. The word used most often in this discussion was indeed "devaluation." A purist economist would rightly claim that it should really be "depreciation," that is, letting the exchange rate float downward freely. We accept the discussion as it was formulated but with this caveat.

2. The main Latvian source is the Bank of Latvia and its governor, Ilmārs Rimšēvičs. Among Western authors, other than one of us (Anders Åslund, "Why Latvia Should Not Devalue," Real Time Economic Issues Watch, Peterson Institute for International Economics, December 9, 2008, www.piie.com), only two defended the policy not to devalue, namely Mary Stokes ("Devaluation in Latvia: Why Not?" RGE Monitor, December 31, 2008); and Christoph Rosenberg ("Why the IMF Supports the Latvian Currency Peg," RGE Monitor, January 6, 2009).

3. Åslund, "Why Latvia Should Not Devalue."

4. DELFI, "Rimshevich podtverdil: devalvatsii ne budet" ["Rimshevich Confirmed: There Will Be No Devaluation"], October 17, 2008, www.delfi.lv.

5. International Monetary Fund, Republic of Latvia, "Request for Stand-By Arrangement," December 19, 2008, 10, www.imf.org (accessed on November 15, 2010).

6. Stokes, "Devaluation in Latvia: Why Not?"

7. DELFI, "Rimshevich podtverdil: devalvatsii ne budet" ["Rimshevich Confirmed: There Will Be No Devaluation"].

8. Edward Hugh, "Why the IMF's Decision to Agree on a Latvian Bailout Programme without Devaluation Is a Mistake," RGE Monitor, December 22, 2008.

9. Edward Harrison, "Are the Baltics the New Argentina?" July 30, 2008, www.creditwritedowns.com (accessed on December 2, 2010).

10. Paul Krugman, "European Crass Warfare," *New York Times*, December 15, 2008.

11. Paul Krugman, "Latvia Is the New Argentina (Slightly Wonkish)," New York Times blog, December 23, 2008.

12. Hugh, "Why the IMF's Decision to Agree on a Latvian Bailout Programme without Devaluation Is a Mistake"; Nouriel Roubini, "Latvia's Currency Crisis Is a Rerun of Argentina's," *Financial Times*, June 11, 2009, 9; Simon Johnson, "Latvia: Should You Care?" *The Baseline Scenario*, June 5, 2009.

13. Hugh, "Why the IMF's Decision to Agree on a Latvian Bailout Programme without Devaluation Is a Mistake."

14. Ibid.

15. Roubini, "Latvia's Currency Crisis Is a Rerun of Argentina's," 9.

16. Hugh, "Why the IMF's Decision to Agree on a Latvian Bailout Programme without Devaluation Is a Mistake."

17. Michael Hudson, "For States in Crisis, Austerity Is Not the Only Option," *Financial Times*, July 8, 2009, 9.

18. Johnson, "Latvia: Should You Care?"

19. Devesh Kapur and Arvind Subramanian, "Wanted: A Truly International Monetary Fund," *Forbes*, March 29, 2009.

20. Niklas Magnusson, "Rogoff Says Latvia Should Devalue Its Currency," Bloomberg, June 29, 2009.

21. Hugh, "Why the IMF's Decision to Agree on a Latvian Bailout Programme without Devaluation Is a Mistake."

22. Marshall Auerback, "Latvia—the Insanity Continues," Roubini Global Economics, October 12, 2009.

23. Michael Hudson, "Finance Capitalism Hits a Wall: The Oligarchs' Escape Pan—at the Treasury's Expense," February 17, 2009, www.michael-hudson.com (accessed on January 11, 2011).

24. Auerback, "Latvia—the Insanity Continues."

25. Hudson, "For States in Crisis," 9.

26. For example, Jose Antonia Cordero, "The IMF's Stand-by Arrangements and the Economic Downturn in Eastern Europe," Center for Economic Policy Research, September 2009; Mark Weisbrot and Rebecca Ray, "Latvia's Recession: The Cost of Adjustment with an 'Internal Devaluation'," Center for Economic Policy Research, February 2010.

27. Roubini, "Latvia's Currency Crisis Is a Rerun of Argentina's," 9.

28. Ibid.

29. International Monetary Fund, Republic of Latvia, "Request for Stand-By Arrangement," 10.

30. Ibid., 5.

31. A longer elaboration on this theme is Anders Åslund, *The Last Shall Be the First: The East European Financial Crisis, 2008–10* (Washington: Peterson Institute for International Economics, 2010, 60–65).

32. Steve Hanke, "Will Dr. Gloom and Dr. Doom's Latvian Domino Fall?" *GlobeAsia*, August 2009, 28.

33. Michael Mussa, *Argentina and the Fund: From Triumph to Tragedy* (Washington: Institute for International Economics, 2002, 51).

34. Mussa, *Argentina and the Fund*, 27.

35. Tony Barber, "Let's Shorten Latvia's Pain," *Financial Times*, June 15, 2010.

36. Christoph Rosenberg, "Why the IMF Supports the Latvian Currency Peg," RGE Monitor, January 6, 2009.

37. Rosenberg, "Why the IMF Supports the Latvian Currency Peg," RGE Monitor, January 6, 2009. Reprinted with permission.

38. International Monetary Fund, "Republic of Latvia 2010 Article IV Consultation," IMF Country Report no. 10/356 (Washington, December 2010).

39. Ibid.

5

Implementation of the Stabilization Program, 2009

After Latvia reached its agreements with the International Monetary Fund (IMF) and the European Commission in December 2008, the government was supposed to implement its commitments, but instead a complex political drama ensued. The center-right opposition and President Valdis Zatlers questioned the competence of the Ivars Godmanis government, which was riddled by infighting, and demonstrations of public discontent on January 13, 2009, shook the country.

The obvious alternative was a slightly different center-right coalition. On March 12, such a government was formed under one of us (Valdis Dombrovskis) with New Era in the lead. As the economic situation had deteriorated, the new government had to redo the budget for 2009, which took two months.

In June 2009, Latvia faced its most serious devaluation crisis. The IMF doubted that Latvia had its public finances under control or could maintain its peg. The European Commission took the lead and issued its more substantial disbursement in early July, with the IMF following belatedly.

Collapse of the Godmanis Government

After the IMF agreement was concluded and international financing secured, the government was supposed to urgently implement the stabilization program. Instead a strange hiatus occurred. Public fury against Parex Bank and the government lingered. Latvians realized that great economic sacrifices were required and questioned the credibility and competence of the government.

The first two months of 2009 seemed somewhat surreal, as the severe economic crisis turned ever worse. By January 30, Swedbank announced that Latvia's GDP was likely to plummet by 10 percent in 2009. It was evident to all that the economy had entered a far sharper fall, but few economic measures were implemented because of political strife. Latvia badly needed a new, more forceful government.

Since mid-December 2008 the government had been preoccupied with a proposal to reduce the number of ministries from 16 to 11 or 12. All government parties favored some streamlining, but each coalition partner had its own preferences. Godmanis started criticizing his ministers for not being very effective, but the public concluded that he was the one making all decisions of significance. Godmanis appeared exhausted, and malaise and discord in the government were palpable. On January 12, 2009 the minister of culture gave up and resigned.

On January 13, some liberal politicians (Society for Different Politics), together with some other organizations and trade unions, organized a large demonstration in Riga, protesting against the government. The organizers demanded that President Zatlers dissolve the parliament because of the government's inability to handle the economic crisis. The peaceful demonstration, which had been planned for a couple of weeks, gathered some 12,000 people. At its end, however, a couple of hundred youth started rioting. Two dozen people were injured and 106 were arrested. These were the worst riots in Latvia since its renewed independence in 1991. The Latvians, who saw themselves as peaceful and democratic, got scared. The organizers of the demonstration instantly called off any future protests.

The protesters had directed their demands to President Zatlers, who was happy to pick up the torch. The next day, he made a public speech on television with three ultimatums to the parliament: (1) vote through amendments to the constitution before March 31 to make it easier to dissolve the parliament, (2) revise the election law so that popular personalities could not pull unknown people into parliament, and (3) form a council to supervise the economic recovery plan and the utilization of state credits. Finally, Zatlers demanded that the government appoint a new head of the controversial Corruption Prevention and Combating Bureau (KNAB), a position that had been vacant since the summer of 2008. His bottom line was: "Trust in the government and officials has collapsed."[1] If the parliament failed to deliver on these demands, President Zatlers threatened to call an early parliamentary election. While according to the Constitution this would require complicated procedures including a referendum, the opposition supported the idea of early elections.

After Zatlers' speech, it was only a matter of time before the increasingly unpopular Godmanis government fell. A mid-January opinion poll showed that 70 percent of the electorate did not trust the government, and 86 percent did not have confidence in the parliament, while 64 percent was ready to vote for the dissolution of the parliament.[2] The unpopular coalition parties had every reason to try to escape early elections, but saying so would have implied weakness, so most claimed: "It is impossible to escape early elections this year."[3]

Meanwhile, tensions continued to develop within the governing coalition. On February 3, following farmers' protests in Riga, the minister of agriculture resigned. Meanwhile Godmanis continued to argue with People's Party about how many ministries the government should have. On February 13, President Zatlers declared: "Prime Minister Ivars Godmanis has lost my confidence."[4] The next day, People's Party said the same. On February 20, Godmanis finally resigned after the two biggest coalition parties, People's Party and the Union of Greens and Farmers, withdrew their support. The government was criticized for corruption and arrogance.[5] No specific force brought down the government. It collapsed because of minimal popular support. Most of all, the government did not seem up to resolving the financial crisis.

Formation of the Dombrovskis Government

It turned out to be relatively easy to form a new government. New Era benefited from having been out of the government and having opposed Godmanis' stabilization program as insufficient. Immediately after Godmanis resigned, it seized the opportunity to call for a broad coalition government to deal with the crisis. The first issue was to find a prime minister. When Godmanis was nominated in 2007, the alternative candidates were Edgars Zalans of People's Party and myself, while the Union of Greens and Farmers did not put forward any candidate. Now, New Era declared me as their candidate, and the rest of the center-right opposition supported me as well. On February 26, President Zatlers handed the formation of a new government to me.

Only three weeks after Godmanis' resignation, on March 12, I was sworn in as prime minister. At the time, I was a member of the European Parliament from New Era, and I had been minister of finance from 2002 to 2004.

Lars Christensen of Danske Bank commented: "Overall, we see this as slightly positive. Early elections are avoided—at least for now—and New Era is normally perceived as relatively reformist. ...As Finance Minister of Latvia [in] 2002–2004, Dombrovskis became known as a classical liberal and fiscally conservative politician. Furthermore, he has been highly critical of the 'boom-bust' economics we have seen in Latvia in recent years."[6]

The composition of the coalition government was almost-given. A broader coalition was required, including the three big center-right parties, New Era, People's Party, and the Union of Greens and Farmers, as well as two small center-right Latvian parties—Civic Union and For Fatherland and Freedom/Latvia's National Independence movement. Altogether, the new government coalition held 64 out of 100 seats in the parliament. Negotiations with Latvia's First Party/Latvia's Way were not successful, and they went into opposition. Harmony Center was barred from the government and abandoned its rather responsible policies for a more populist line, which was to last through the elections in October 2010. It called for reducing the value-added tax (VAT) to 12 percent and cutting the "army of civil servants."[7]

New Era took pride in its economic competence and received the three most important positions for economic policy in the government. Former prime minister and former central bank governor Einars Repše was given the post of minister of finance and Artis Kampars minister of economy. The number of ministries was reduced moderately from 16 to 14. Few expected this government to survive for long. The Latvian media even called me the "Kamikaze Prime Minister."[8] A spokesman for Harmony Center warned that I would "drown like a horse."[9] At 37 I was the youngest prime minister in Latvia's history. Because of the formation of a new government with greater popular and parliamentary support, the question of early elections gradually faded away. The next ordinary elections were scheduled for early October 2010. After the new government had been confirmed, popular support for New Era rose from 6.6 to 10.2 percent, which calmed the political situation.[10]

The dynamics of economic policymaking changed with the new government. Central bank governor Ilmārs Rimšēvičs was a constant force who in nearly every public statement insisted on the fixed exchange rate and a budget deficit below the Maastricht ceiling of 3 percent of GDP in 2012 to qualify for euro adoption in 2014. In the previous government, Prime Minister Godmanis had been the financial micromanager. Now Repše took the lead on fiscal restructuring—the customary role of a minister of finance—becoming the fiscal hardliner who usually proposed greater cuts than anybody else. Minister of Economy Kampars lent Repše support. Against these two New Era ministers stood the ministers of health care, social welfare, and regional development from People's Party, who lobbied for their interest groups and opposed drastic cuts. The prime minister had the traditional role of moderator within the government, though I leaned in favor of financial stabilization. The new government was reasonably balanced and functioned normally.

Meanwhile, the economic situation deteriorated fast, but more realistic assessments of the severity of the crisis emerged. In late February, one local investment banker, Girts Rungainis, claimed that GDP would fall by 12 percent in 2009 and presciently that unemployment would rise to 21.7 percent (marginally higher than the actual peak).[11]

In late February, the IMF and the European Commission declared publicly that they were taking a break in their negotiations with Latvia until a new government was formed. Because of the economic crisis, the IMF demanded that all budget expenditures be cut by 20 percent from the planned level for 2009. In March 2009, the IMF was supposed to issue its second tranche, but it was dissatisfied with Latvia's fiscal performance, as the crisis undermined state revenues and boosted social expenditures. The IMF mission found that Latvia did not deserve a second tranche of €200 million because the necessary budget amendments had not been drafted.[12] The IMF suspended lending to Latvia until June when a new budget was adopted with more cuts in public spending.[13]

In March, financial markets were further jolted and two crisis indicators peaked. The yields on Latvian eurobonds due in 2018 surged to 12 percent a year. The credit default swap rates for five-year default insurance peaked on

March 10, 2009, at 1,193 basis points (figure 5.1). However, as the new government started elaborating its economic policy, its public declarations were sufficient to calm financial markets.

A New Stabilization Program Takes Shape

The new government was more determined to stabilize the economy than its predecessor, although two oligarchic parties participated in the coalition. Repše stated in no uncertain terms: "We will stabilize the financial situation, get the planned budget cuts done and increase efficiency and transparency."[14] I emphasized that Latvia had no choice but to fulfill its obligations to the IMF so that the country could receive international financial aid.[15]

The immediate task was to restore the financial stability of the country. My first public comment after being assigned the task of forming a new government was that Latvia was on the verge of bankruptcy and immediate action was needed to restore financial stability. Without further international loans, reserves in the treasury would have lasted only a few months. The real reason for the collapse of the Godmanis government was its unwillingness to deal with the additional hugely unpopular budget cuts necessary to fulfill IMF and European Commission requirements and continue receiving installments of the international loan.

Given that three parties from the previous coalition government were also in the new government, it was important to ensure their support for additional budget cuts. Therefore in addition to the regular documents that are drafted while forming a government (e.g., government's declaration and coalition agreement), a "memorandum on immediate measures to ensure the solvency of the state" was prepared with the support of the Ministry of Finance and contained a range of specific measures to reduce the 2009 budget deficit below 7 percent of GDP. All coalition members of parliament signed the memorandum to ensure their support prior to the vote on the new government. In March 2009 it was obvious that the macroeconomic situation was much worse than projected, and the original program target of below 5 percent of GDP for the 2009 budget deficit was out of reach. Therefore the memorandum set a new target of 7 percent of GDP. Although I held some preliminary consultations with the IMF and the European Commission about this target, it was still to be officially negotiated (later a target of 10 percent of GDP was agreed on).

In a press conference on March 23, I elaborated on the position of the new government.[16] The situation was severe and getting worse: "The forecast for the recession right now is [a GDP decline of] 12 percent and in fact it may get worse as we will introduce additional austerity measures in the State Budget." The "previous Government had committed itself to reduce public sector salaries by some 15 percent, freeze pensions, and take a number of other austerity measures,...but it left without even attempting to deal with the budget amendments." The aggravated situation called for further cuts: "Very unpopular

Figure 5.1 Credit default swap rates, 2008–10

5-year, basis points

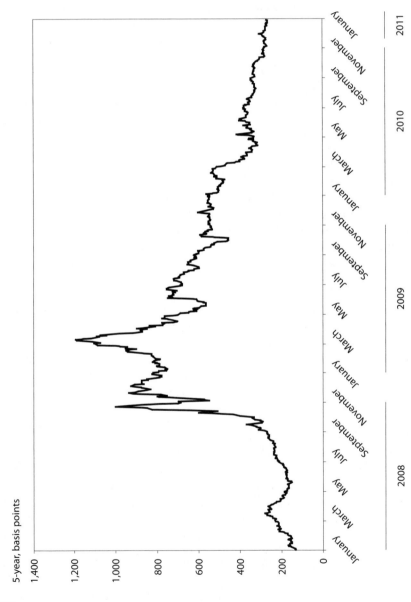

Source: Thomson DataStream.

measures will be necessary, no doubt about it. The question is: Do we have any choice? In the current situation..., we do not have many choices." Yet the general policy line remained the same, with full commitment to the fixed exchange rate to the euro, large public expenditure cuts as necessary for financial stabilization, and austerity measures to reform the public sector.

In two regards, the new government differed from its predecessor. First, it emphasized that the policy should be equitable and properly explained to the people:

> Once you carry out budget cuts, people expect them to be applied also to the rich. The previous Government was not willing to undertake certain measures; for example, we dismantled boards of public companies that were subject to criticism as a source of income for people from political parties. We significantly reduced salaries for executive boards of public companies. [Contrary] to the previous government, we also reduced the salaries of ministers and other top officials within the government. We will ensure that the cuts do not apply only to policemen, teachers or the health care sector.[17]

Another distinction the new government wanted to make was that it was not going to get lost pursuing illusory measures, such as government reorganization, but focus on essentials, such as budget policy:

> For two weeks the previous government argued whether there would be 11 or 12 ministries and then the government collapsed. Later Ivars Godmanis admitted that his government did not collapse due to this ministry issue but because of the budget amendments. So we are not entering into this debate on 11 or 12 ministries. Our coalition agreed on 14 ministries....[18]

But were the necessary budget cuts really possible? My response was: "The whole task is close to impossible.... First the immediate cuts should be implemented fairly quickly to ensure the solvency of the state. The second step is fundamental structural reforms, which we can implement by 2010."[19]

But there were also two pieces of good news. "First of all, in January [2009], for the first time in many years we had a positive current account balance."[20] Second, the new state management of Parex Bank had successfully refinanced its syndicated loans and no other bank failures occurred. In mid-April, the Latvian government signed an agreement with the European Bank for Reconstruction and Development (EBRD) on the sale of 25 percent plus one share of Parex Bank, giving the Latvian government a strong and competent[21] partner in dealing with this complex problem. Latvia would need only about one-quarter of the €2.7 billion granted in credits for bank stabilization, and it would not need any additional loans in spite of the deteriorating economic situation.[22] On the eve of assuming office, I predicted that the standard of living would start improving in the second half of 2010,[23] which luckily turned out to be the case.

The government devoted April and May to preparatory work for crisis resolution. The GDP forecasts for 2009 were steadily revised downward until the end of May, when it became clear how profound the Latvian economic crisis was. GDP had plummeted by no less than 18 percent in the first quarter of 2009, and the former IMF mission chief, Christoph Rosenberg, assessed that GDP could fall by a similar amount for the year as a whole,[23] which turned out to be the actual number.

Therefore, the Ministry of Finance had to anticipate an even greater fall in state revenues, which necessitated larger budget cuts. These cuts would have to be more uneven, as some activities had to be shielded. Latvia needed a new budget based on completely new principles, and it could be ready only in early June.[24] If Latvia were forced into default, draconian measures, such as a budget without deficit, would become necessary. Therefore, the government had to opt for sufficient budget cuts.[25]

The starting point was to include sufficient measures in the supplementary budget since it would be more difficult to introduce additional cuts later. Second, public expenditure cuts were preferable to higher taxes. Alberto Alesina and Silvia Ardagna have offered substantial statistical evidence for the thesis: "Fiscal stimuli...based upon spending cuts and no tax increases are more likely to reduce deficits and debt over GDP ratios than those based upon tax increases."[26] Third, the fiscal cuts should not be even but aim at structural reforms improving the public sector. Fourth, in both design and promotion, the government had to try to explain austerity so that the public understood and accepted it.

The total fiscal adjustment was huge. In December 2008, the Godmanis government had adopted total cuts of 7 percent of GDP, although many had not been implemented. The new government added fiscal adjustment of 4 percent of GDP (8 percent of GDP in annual terms since this was in the middle of the year), adding to a total of 11 percent of GDP for 2009.

The government asked the ministries to prepare structural reforms for three alternative scenarios with public expenditure cuts of 20, 30, and 40 percent and salary decreases of an average of 20 percent.[27] A couple of ministers, for social welfare and health care, protested publicly against Repše's planned budget cuts. Characteristically, Repše responded by suggesting further cuts. Even when reducing public expenditures and salaries by 20 percent in the middle of the year, he assessed that the 2009 budget deficit would be 8.5 percent of GDP.[28]

The government targeted three sectors for far-reaching structural reforms, namely public administration, health care, and education. I demanded that the minister of health care cut the ministerial staff by 44 percent, pointing out that the health care administration employed only 400 people in Estonia, whereas Latvia employed as many as 1,500 (Latvia's population was three-quarters larger, which would have justified only 700 employees, but I proposed to leave it at 840).[29]

Such international comparisons became the hallmark of the new government. Rather than just cutting by a standard rate, the government tried to find an international norm that made sense and on that basis pursued profound structural reforms within each institution. Luckily, the government did not have to invent these reforms hastily. They were well prepared and documented, primarily through studies the government had done with the World Bank. The government basically had to take these reform proposals off the shelf and start implementing them, and it did. The overarching priority for structural reform was to restore the country's competitiveness, which had two dimensions: in the short term, improving Latvia's credit ratings and access to finance for enterprises, and in the long run increasing the efficiency of Latvia's economy.

Latvia already had a Master Plan on Optimization of the Hospital Network. A country of 2.2 million, Latvia had far too many hospitals—a Soviet inheritance of more hospital beds than medical care. Therefore, the government decided to close 35 of 59 hospitals by 2013 to the benefit of the people's health. Latvia would still have 24 hospitals, which was plenty by any international standard.[30]

The situation was similar in education. Given that the population had declined by 15 percent since independence, and birth rates remained low, Latvia had too many schools and teachers. It had one teacher for every seven students—the highest in Europe—compared with a European average of one teacher per 12 students. In order to encourage savings and efficiency, the government introduced the principle that education funding should be based on a fixed amount per pupil for each category. That would encourage downsizing of the school network and raise the pupil-to-teacher ratio to a reasonable level. More than 100 schools were closed, and 2,400 teachers were laid off.[31] Similarly, Latvia had too many institutions of higher learning, and none of them outstanding, suggesting the need for rationalization and quality improvement and better use of tuition fees.

Unfortunately, during the boom years these reforms were too politically unpopular to be implemented. The new government had to accelerate the pace of these reforms during the recession, as reform starts where the money ends. The government attracted a lot of public attention when it started reducing the number of teachers, schools, and hospitals. But rather than stopping, the government proceeded to other fields to show that it was even-handed as well as serious about rationalization.

Administrative reforms were politically much easier, because most people wanted fewer bureaucrats. The government initiated a substantial downsizing and streamlining of the state apparatus. Half of the 75 state agencies were to be closed down and 8,000 civil servants to be laid off initially.[32] Eventually, no fewer than 23,000 or 29 percent of the civil servants were dismissed, as their total number was reduced from 87,500 in the third quarter of 2008 to 62,300 in the second quarter of 2010 (figure 5.2). The reduction in bureaucracy also eased the hardship of citizens.

Another popular reform was to limit the salaries of the members of boards of corporations with state ownership. No fewer than 73 parliamentarians voted for this law, and none against.[33] A third appreciated measure was to set a

Figure 5.2 Number of public employees, quarterly, 2008–10

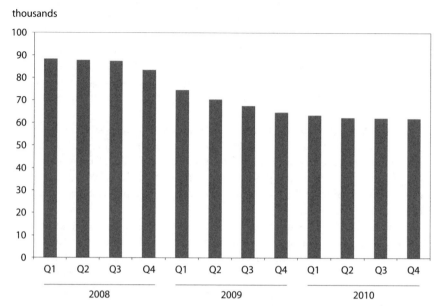

thousands

Source: Central Statistical Bureau of Latvia, www.csb.gov.lv (accessed on March 7, 2011).

ceiling for the salaries of managers of state corporations, not to mention that 1,000 out of the 5,000 employees of the State Revenue Service were let go.[34] Each of these measures might not have saved much money, but they showed that the government was serious about distributing the cost of adjustment also to the privileged.

Wage cuts were widespread throughout the public and private sectors from the beginning of 2009. To begin with, average public salaries were substantially higher than private salaries, but by the end of 2009 only insignificantly so. The average public salary actually fell by 26 percent from November 2008 to November 2009 (figure 5.3).[35] Private salaries declined by "only" 10 percent. Then both private and public salaries stayed stagnant through 2010. Although these salary cuts were substantial, they were lower than official policy required, while anecdotal evidence suggests that salary decreases of 15 to 20 percent were common in private firms in Riga. Presumably, the highly paid, well-to-do middle class faced larger salary cuts than poorer workers who had never flourished. Another explanation is probably that fringe benefits never entered the official statistics, and they were abandoned first. Thus there are reasons to suspect that the real wage reduction in the private sector was somewhat greater than statistics show.

A rise in unemployment was inevitable, but it was stark. Unemployment surged from a low of 6.6 percent in the second quarter of 2008 to a high

Figure 5.3   Gross average monthly salaries in public and private sectors, 2008–10

lats

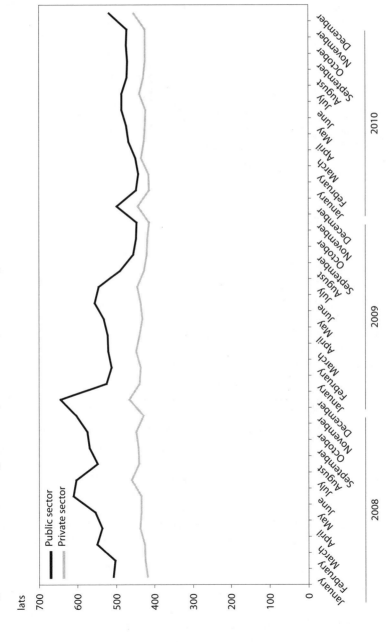

Note: 1 lat = approximately US$2.

Source: Central Statistical Bureau of Latvia, www.csb.gov.lv (accessed on March 3, 2011).

75

Figure 5.4 Quarterly unemployment rate, 2008–10

percent of labor force

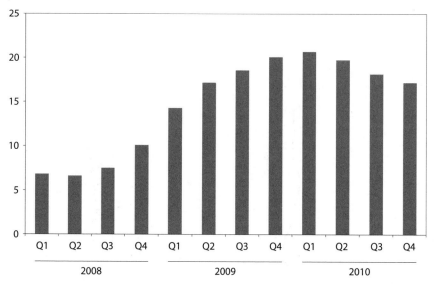

Source: Central Statistical Bureau of Latvia, www.csb.gov.lv (accessed on March 3, 2011).

of 20.7 percent in the first quarter of 2010, after which it started declining (figure 5.4). With little doubt, the sharp rise in unemployment was the worst social effect of the Latvian financial crisis. The government responded by extending unemployment benefits.

This fiscal consolidation package was a large fiscal antistimulus in the midst of the recession, and the government needed to do something to stimulate the economy, but means were scarce. The EU grant funds—the EU Structural Funds, the European Social Fund, and the Cohesion Fund—were the only significant source of such financing (see box 5.1). These EU funds could be used for various purposes but conditions were attached to some of them, notably that the recipient government had to maintain matching funds. The Latvian government maintained and even increased matching funds for EU infrastructure projects to accelerate the absorption of the EU funds. In June 2009, a new export credits guarantee program was started.

In addition to supporting entrepreneurship and export-oriented industries, the government allocated EU grant funding to social welfare programs. In the fall of 2009, it introduced a minimum social safety network in cooperation with the World Bank to improve targeted social support to those members of society in the greatest need. Funding from the European Social Fund was instrumental in mitigating unemployment, facilitating a large temporary works program involving tens of thousands of people. The government extended

Box 5.1   Intricacies of EU financing

The impact of the European Union on its new member countries has been great and multiple. In the 1990s, the candidate countries benefited from greater market access to the vast European market. As the accession process became serious, they were required to adopt all the rules and regulations of the now 125,000 pages of legal text in the *acquis communautaire*. Most of it was beneficial improvement of legislation.

With accession, a tremendous integration of trade and investment occurred, which contributed to high economic growth but also to the financial bubble. Entering the Exchange Rate Mechanism (ERM II) in 2005, Latvia endeavored to follow the fiscal Maastricht criteria or the Stability and Growth Pact (SGP) more seriously than the euro area countries, because it had to comply with the convergence criteria to be allowed to adopt the euro, but inflation soared beyond control.

The European Union was a source of not only emergency loans—which we discuss at length in this chapter—but also very substantial flows of various grants. When Latvia became a member of the European Union, three EU funds, the Cohesion Fund, the European Social Fund, and European Regional Development Fund, became available to it. For 2007–13, Latvia was allocated a substantial total amount of €4.5 billion. These funds support multiple activities in Latvia, such as infrastructure projects in the fields of transportation, environmental protection, and energy (including energy efficiency), as well as public works for the unemployed and improvement of administrative capacity.[1]

A member country pays about 1 percent of GDP to the common EU budget, and so does Latvia. In 2009, it received 4 percent of GDP in return, and these funds were not credits but grants. The government realized that it had not utilized all the EU funding opportunities as it should have. Therefore, it focused on raising these revenues from 4 percent of GDP in 2009 to 7.4 percent of GDP in 2010.[2]

Most EU funding requires the recipient government to provide matching funds, so while public capital funding was reduced by half, that cofinanced by the EU was maintained. Thus, the IMF program of July 2010 contained substantial commitments to increased expenditures.[3] The government's focus on EU financing paid off handsomely. The flow of EU grants into Latvia grew steadily during the financial crisis, and this less discussed issue is one reason why Latvia did so much better than many expected.

---

1. European Commission, "European Cohesion Policy in Latvia: Cohesion Policy 2007–13," 2009, http://ec.europa.eu (accessed on January 22, 2011).

2. International Monetary Fund, Republic of Latvia, "Third Review under the Stand-By Arrangement and Financing Assurances Review," July 6, 2010, 26-27, www.imf.org.

3. Ibid., 44.

unemployed benefits and increased guaranteed minimum income benefits for those who no longer qualified for unemployment benefits. It improved accessibility of health care and medicines to poor people and provided some support for local governments affected by school reform. It started cofinancing local governments' spending on guaranteed minimum income benefit and housing benefit. Thus, the minimum social safety network helped the most vulnerable parts of society.[36]

The government also focused on social dialogue. It created a reform management group, together with representatives of employers' organizations, trade unions, and local governments, while preparing proposals for the 2009 budget amendments and the 2010 budget. These painful budget cuts were actually agreed to by the new government, employers, trade unions, and local governments. Some parties later regretted this agreement, but it had already been written and signed. Key social partners were on board with the government at the critical time, which helped maintain social stability.

In March–May 2009, the government also made extensive efforts to shore up diplomatic support for the credibility and financing of Latvia's stabilization program. In the course of about a month, I met with German Chancellor Angela Merkel, European Commission President José Manuel Barroso, EU Commissioner for Economic and Monetary Affairs Joaquin Almunia, and Swedish Prime Minister Frederik Reinfeldt. Other steady allies were the other Baltic and Nordic countries and select East European countries, such as Poland.

To sum up, the main aspects of the new government's work were fiscal consolidation, structural reform, economic stimulus to the extent the country could afford it, a social safety network and social dialogue to ensure social stability, and diplomacy to maintain international financial support. This combination seemed to work. The public discussion focused on the concrete anticrisis measures rather than on general criticism of the policy. However, some people within, and especially outside, Latvia said that this program, regardless of the details, would not work, because they had concluded that Latvia had to devalue to solve its problems.

Devaluation Crisis, But Adoption of a New Budget, June 2009

The Latvian stabilization drama came to a head in June 2009, when everything was supposed to unfold, and the stakes were high. It was time for the government to prove itself. It had announced that it would present a supplementary budget for 2009 to be approved by parliament in order to ensure continuation of the international loan program. That month, the European Commission was scheduled to provide the largest tranche of its financing, €1.2 billion, and the IMF was supposed to deliver its second tranche of €200 million. Without this funding, Latvia would have been in a tight financial squeeze on both its international reserves and budget financing. In early June, Latvia's international reserves hit their nadir of only €2,644 million (figure 5.5). The starkest crisis indicator was the domestic market interest rates. The Riga three-month interest rate began sharply rising in June (peaking on June 26 at 29.8 percent a year) (figure 5.6).

June was therefore the critical month for everything to come together. The Latvian government needed to have a viable budget adopted in June and on its basis receive international financing, but vociferous calls for devaluation kept thwarting this process. These unwarranted predictions triggered two devaluation scares in Latvia—one at the beginning and the other at the end of this dramatic month.

Andris Šķēle, the former prime minister and leader of the People's Party, the biggest party in the ruling coalition, argued repeatedly that a reduction of incomes of the population was more unpleasant than devaluation of the lat.[37] He enjoyed considerable personal authority since he had been prime minister during 1995–97 and after the Russian financial crisis, 1999–2000. In early June, the powerful Ventspils Mayor Aivars Lembergs made one public comment that the stable lat was killing Latvia's industry, so it had to be devalued.[38]

But the statement on June 1 by the former governor of the Swedish Riksbank, Bengt Dennis, came as a blow to the government. He said on Swedish television that the issue was not if but when Latvia would devalue. A member of the High-Level Advisors Group to the Government of Latvia, his words received wide publicity, making it appear to be the view of the government. But he had taken the government by surprise, and I immediately clarified that the opinion expressed by Dennis "about an inevitable devaluation of the Latvian national currency—lats—is not true, and...has nothing to do... with the position of the government of Latvia on overcoming the economic crisis" and reemphasized the government's commitment to "a stable national currency."[39] Dennis resigned from the advisors group after this incident.

Numerous international economists chimed in that Latvia had to devalue. On June 9, the prominent economist Nouriel Roubini argued in the *Financial Times* that the Latvian stabilization policy was self-defeating, as "devaluation seems unavoidable."[40] Later in June, Kenneth Rogoff, a former IMF chief economist, claimed that the IMF made the wrong decision when it allowed Latvia to keep its currency peg and that it should have been forced to devalue and default on its debt.[41]

In the midst of this drama, on June 6, Latvia held both local and European Parliament elections. Most important were the local elections to the councils in Latvia's nine cities and 109 counties. The changes were limited. The most significant outcome might have been that Harmony Center won 34 percent of the votes in Riga city, and its leader, Nils Ušakovs, became the first ethnic Russian mayor of Riga in the city's 800-year history. Moreover, Latvia's First Party/Latvia's Way received 15 percent of the votes in Riga, and Ainārs Šlesers, the outspoken opponent of New Era, became deputy mayor of Riga. The city administration of the capital was outside of government control.[42]

Figure 5.5 Foreign currency reserves, monthly, 2009–10

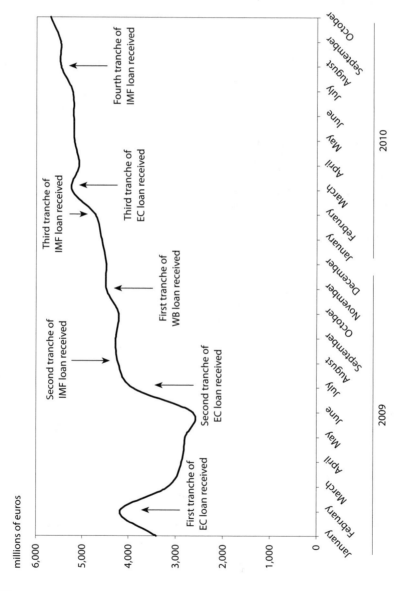

millions of euros

EC = European Commission; IMF = International Monetary Fund; WB = World Bank

Source: Bank of Latvia, www.bank.lv (accessed on December 5, 2010).

Figure 5.6 Market interest rates, 2008–10

percent per annum

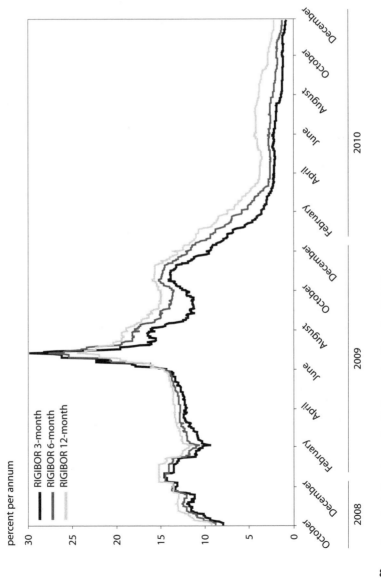

Source: Bank of Latvia, www.bank.lv (accessed on November 23, 2010).

In the European Parliament elections, Civic Union won with 24.3 percent of the votes, showcasing its popular candidates, and Harmony Center came second with 19.6 percent. New Era came sixth with only 6.7 percent, but as it was closely allied with Civic Union, this was no big blow to New Era. Neither of the two big oligarchic government parties, People's Party or the Union of Greens and Farmers, received any seat, which was probably the most significant outcome.[43] Both elections amounted to a minor loss for the government but had no impact on policy.

In the meantime, the forecasts of economic contraction in 2009 had been gradually revised downward from a GDP decline of 5 percent in December 2008 to 12 percent in March and 18 percent in June. The government estimated that the central government deficit would be 8.2 percent of GDP in 2009, to which a local government deficit of 1 percent of GDP would have to be added, making a total budget deficit of 9.2 percent of GDP. This budget deficit was much larger than the 5 percent of GDP that the IMF had accepted, but that had been in December 2008, and the economic decline had been far worse than predicted.

The government responded to all these challenges with a flurry of activity, trying to quickly decide on sufficient measures and convince multiple constituencies of their necessity. On June 1, the government adopted its budget amendments for 2009. On June 4, I presented them to an extraordinary session of the parliament for the first reading, warning that they amounted to "unprecedented austerity measures." The three key aims were to overcome the financial crisis, safeguard social needs, and boost economic growth through structural reforms to be implemented over two to five years.[44] However, the IMF and European Commission deemed the government's proposals for the first reading insufficient and requested more cuts for the second reading.

The proposed measures were draconian. Public salaries would be cut for a second time by about 20 percent and other public expenditures by 40 percent, with some exception for education, health care, justice, and public order. The only good news was that no further VAT increases were required for the moment.[45] Structural reforms that had not as yet been elaborated were planned for 2010 and 2011.[46]

Still, many public expenditures could not be cut, notably contributions to the European Union, North Atlantic Treaty Organization (NATO), United Nations, and other international organizations. The government had to service its debt, and EU funds could not be received without matching government funds. Latvia refused to stop its engagement in Afghanistan because of solidarity with the United States and NATO. Unemployment benefits inevitably rose with unemployment.[47]

An obvious question was whether the government had a plan B if the international lenders decided not to make any further payments. My natural response was: "We must focus on plan A—to ensure that we receive the international loan. A plan B would be very insufficient. It is important to understand that the IMF is the lender of last resort. It is usually approached by countries that cannot borrow anywhere else."[48] A month earlier, in May, I had clarified to a group of international journalists: "There are two options. One is making unpopular cuts in order to obtain further loan payments from international lenders. The second option is making many more unpopular cuts anyway by the end of June. So it is not a question of how willing we are but of what options we have."[49]

The government also responded to the devaluation predictions, calling for public responsibility. I particularly addressed "those making unfounded statements concerning the stability of the Latvian national currency. These announcements damage the Latvian economy and may adversely affect our adoption of the euro.... To those who think of devaluation as a miracle solution I would like to say that this solution would [be] much more costly to the economy and society than the proposed...budget amendments.... Devaluation would have an impact on everyone, and the bad experiences of many countries show that quite often it is beyond control."[50]

Adding to the already tense situation were rumors of the government's resignation. They were so rampant that I felt compelled to make a public statement on June 11 that no such resignation had taken place and that it was not even considered.[51]

The same day, the government concluded an agreement between the five coalition parties and the government's social partners, the Employers' Confederation, the Free Trade Union Confederation, the Association of Local and Regional Governments, the Chamber of Commerce and Industry, and the Federation of Pensioners. It was fairly detailed and far-reaching, specifying measures for a budget deficit reduction of 500 million lats (4 percent of 2009 GDP or 8 percent of GDP in annual terms). Both President Zatlers and Bank of Latvia Governor Rimšēvičs participated in drafting the agreement. It focused on the state bureaucracy. State-owned corporations were obligated to contribute 80 percent of their profits in dividends to the state budget. The central administration of the ministries had to reduce their expenditures by 30 percent, and the number of state agencies and their administrative expenditures were to be cut by 50 percent. Each ministry was assigned specific reduction targets.

Pensions and family allowances were to decrease by 10 percent, and pensions for working pensioners by no less than 70 percent.[52] The Pensioners' Federation signed the agreement with some reservations. No attempt was made to raise Latvia's low retirement age of 62 years, because it would not give much short-term saving and made little sense at a time of high and rising unemployment. In taxation, the agreement included a substantial reduction of the personal income tax exemption and an increase in some excise taxes.

The negotiations over this agreement lasted well past midnight and feelings were mixed. These measures were unprecedentedly harsh, but they would be sufficient to ensure continued international financial support so that the nation could escape the much more dire scenario of default. After the coalition party leaders signed this agreement with the social partners, they could do little but vote for the budget. On June 16, the Latvian parliament approved the budget cuts the European Union and the IMF had demanded.[53]

The new budget deficit targets agreed to with the European Union and the IMF were 10 percent of GDP for the 2009 budget and 8.5 percent of GDP for the 2010 budget. The targets were set on the basis of the European System of Accounts of 1995 (ESA95) methodology and excluded bank restructuring costs. As measured by ESA95, the budget deficit tends to be slightly larger than measured in cash flow terms, usually around 1.5 percent of GDP, but the difference varies. As cash flows are more easily measured, the first numbers available are given in cash flow, while the more accurate ESA95 numbers become available much later, which contributed to budget disputes.

The Latvian government agreed with the European Union and the IMF on fiscal adjustments of 500 million lats ($1 billion) both in budget amendments for 2009 and for the 2010 budget. At that time a fiscal adjustment of 500 million lats was thought to be consistent with a 2010 budget deficit target of 8.5 percent of GDP. But this setting of double targets for 2010 backfired later. The actual outcome of the 2009 general government budget deficit was 6.8 percent of GDP in cash terms and 10.2 percent of GDP in ESA95 terms (9.3 percent of GDP excluding bank restructuring costs).

Despite all the apocalyptic predictions of devaluation, no real run on foreign reserves occurred. Technically, that could have happened only if the Latvian people pulled out their bank deposits and exchanged them into foreign currency, because the Latvian economy is so small, its financial sector tiny, and lats were rarely used. The financial market is really very thin. Eighty-seven percent of all loans in the Latvian economy were made in euros. In June 2009, Latvia's international reserves were about $4.1 billion, almost equaling total bank deposits in lats of $4.2 billion. In addition, $1.65 billion of lats in cash were in circulation. The reserves were sufficient to guarantee stability.[54] Few other financial assets denominated in lats could be sold short. Total outstanding government bonds in lats were only $1.9 billion. The stock market was minuscule, with a daily turnover of a mere $200,000. In early June 2009, bankers in Riga said privately that speculators offered 10 percent a month to speculate against the lat, but nobody wanted to lend to them because the holders of lats were interested in sustaining the lat. A senior investment banker said privately that their customers only speculated through credit default swaps to avoid counterparty risk. Even so the credit default swap rate fell from a high of 1,100 basis points in March 2009 to a moderate level of 400 basis points by late September, compared with a peak of more than 5,400 basis points for Ukraine in March 2009 (which did not result in default either).

As long as the Latvian people trusted their government enough to not start a bank-and-currency run, nobody could force Latvia to devalue. But after securing a domestic austerity agreement, Latvia needed international financial support very badly.

Complicated IMF-EU Negotiations

Latvia's negotiations with the international lenders are usually described as negotiations with the IMF, but this was not quite accurate, as representatives of the European Commission always point out. The international negotiating team was large and multifaceted. The IMF mission from Washington led the negotiations. Initially, Christoph Rosenberg temporarily headed it but was soon replaced by Mark Griffiths, who was sometimes replaced by his senior Anne-Marie Gulde. The European Commission mission was led by Elena Flores and later by Gabriele Giudice of the Economic and Financial Directorate in Brussels. The IMF and the European Commission functioned as co-chairs. In addition, an official from the Swedish Ministry of Finance, Åke Törnqvist, represented the bilateral lenders. Sometimes, Jens Henriksson, the executive director at the IMF in Washington for the five Nordic and three Baltic countries, participated as well. Other institutions represented in the negotiations were, notably, the World Bank.

These different missions had to report home. The bilateral donors had no routine way of doing this and therefore the most complex system. In each of the four Nordic donor countries, the ministry of finance and the central bank as well as the prime minister's office were continuously involved, and different coordinating meetings were held. The four also had a similar system for their support of Iceland. The common judgment of the senior management involved was that this system was not tenable because it required too much of their time, but that also meant that top policymakers in these countries were greatly involved and lent Latvia keen support.

By June 2009, a serious conflict had emerged between the European Union and the IMF over the Latvian program, involving budget projections and exchange rate policy. After the new budget cuts, the Latvian government assessed its likely budget deficit at 9 percent of GDP. The European Commission accepted the Latvian assertions, while the IMF mission thought the Latvian budget deficit would be far larger. Later, however, the IMF acknowledged that Latvia's actual budget deficit in 2009 was only 7 percent of GDP all in cash-flow terms.[55]

Skeptical of the Latvian budget projections, the IMF mission doubted that the peg could be maintained, while the Latvians, the EU mission, and the bilateral donors all reckoned that the decision about the exchange rate had been made once and for all. The IMF mission suggested repeatedly that the Latvians prepare a "plan B," meaning devaluation, but the Latvians refused because they presumed that any such plan would be easily leaked to the very open Latvian society, destroying the credibility of their peg and causing panic. After all, only Latvian depositors with bank accounts in lats could bring down the exchange rate. A common suspicion among senior Latvian officials was that the IMF wanted to force Latvia to devalue. Officially, the IMF maintained complete silence.

At the IMF headquarters in Washington, the dominant view was that Latvia would eventually have to devalue. The Latvian Stand-By Arrangement was perceived as unsustainable and thus a mistake. Therefore, it was considered better to let Latvia fail early on before the IMF pumped it up with debt, as IMF loans cannot be reduced but have to be repaid in full. Once again a parallel with Argentina was drawn. The IMF top management was conspicuously silent, giving the impression that Latvia had been delegated to mid-level staff.

Originally, the European Union had accepted that the IMF would take the lead in the stabilization program, but now European Commission officials started complaining in private: If the IMF isn't leading, then what is it doing? The Europeans wondered what the IMF was doing with "their" money, because the European Union contributed more money than the IMF in the Latvian program, apart from accounting for roughly one-third of the IMF capital. The European Union no longer accepted the IMF's leadership of the international negotiations. EU Commissioner for Economic and Monetary Affairs Joaquin Almunia adopted an active, high-profile position on Latvia, which was not matched by the IMF management.

On June 19, the European Council, that is, all the heads of the EU member states, made an unusual statement, expressing strong support for further international aid for Latvia:

> The European Council supports the adoption of the new budgetary measures in Latvia aiming at sizeable fiscal consolidation this and next year. It stresses that rigorous implementation of the measures adopted together with credible medium-term strategy is imperative to delivering a successful outcome of the current adjustment programme. The European Council welcomes the intention of the Commission to propose the swift disbursement of the next instalment of the Community balance-of-payment assistance.[56]

Overtly, this seemed an admonition to the Latvian government and the European Commission, but it was also a terse note to the IMF that it had better deliver money to Latvia. The Swedes, the other Nordics, the Balts, and the Poles were the main movers, and they were also represented on the Executive Board of the IMF. Swedish Prime Minister Fredrik Reinfeldt stated publicly: "We think that a clear signal of support from the EU would help them to achieve support from the IMF."[57]

On July 2, the European Union went ahead on its own. It overruled the IMF, giving Latvia a huge second tranche of $1.2 billion, which marked the end of the acute Latvian financial crisis. As a consequence, the IMF no longer held the key to international assistance to Latvia. This experience with the IMF may have contributed to the European Union's reluctance to involve the IMF in a Greek bailout in the first half of 2010.

Finally, on July 27, a doubtful IMF decided to disburse a second tranche.[58] Its decision did not come as a convincing judgment but rather as recognition that it had been overruled by the European Union. Select European governments and the European executive directors had demanded that the IMF issue its second tranche to Latvia, and the IMF preferred to catch up rather than lose face, but it dragged its feet and delayed the disbursement by one month.

With the release of EU funding in July 2009, Latvia had passed the critical phase of the crisis. The country was ready to heal. The disbursement of the EU money boosted the reserves to almost €4 billion in July (figure 5.5), and the foreign reserves scare was over. After that, Latvia's reserves grew steadily though slowly and were no longer an issue. The Bank of Latvia was not forced to intervene to support the lat any more. Credit default swap rates and interest rates continued to fall and normalized by September. Inflation continued to fall by about one percentage point a month. In August, annualized inflation dropped to 1.8 percent from 15.7 percent a year earlier.

The crucial role of the European Union must be underlined. Without its support on July 2, Latvia's situation would have remained critical for no good reason. In hindsight, it is all too obvious that Latvia suffered from a liquidity squeeze and not a solvency problem, and the European Union salvaged it. The persistent absence of the ECB, which could have supplied liquidity through credit swaps, remains a remarkable but not very honorable memory. The perceptive Edward Hugh posed the question: "Are the IMF and the ECB lining up against the EU Commission over Latvia?"[59]

Still, the salient point is that the IMF, the European Union, the World Bank, the European Investment Bank, the EBRD, and the bilateral donors reacted fast and offered substantial amounts of emergency credit when Latvia needed it most. The international creditors have also helped the Latvian government to carry out useful structural reforms that will generate greater welfare in the future. Like the Bank of Latvia and the ministry of finance, they have argued for slightly tighter budgets than Latvia's Cabinet of Ministers did as a whole, but that is normal politics.

From Latvia's point of view, the cooperation between the IMF and the European Commission worked well, but without the European Commission checking the IMF, the international stabilization program could easily have fallen apart in June 2009. For Latvia, it has been an advantage to have both parties at the table rather than one.

The bilateral donors have not had to disburse any funds, but their funding was always meant to be a last resort. Yet, in December 2008, their very real support, which was approved by their parliaments, was vital for the credibility of the international stabilization program. Particular mention should be made of the Nordic bridge credit of €500 million in late 2008. Moreover, it was the bilateral donors that tilted the balance to Latvia's advantage within the European Union in June 2009.

The World Bank, which advised the government's structural reforms, also had an important impact, as did the European Investment Bank, which was the first international institution to support Latvia in October 2008, and the EBRD, which helped with financing and technical support of the restructuring of Parex Bank.

In parallel, on September 11, 2009, the EBRD and the IMF organized a meeting with the four main foreign banks with subsidiaries in Latvia (Swedbank, SEB, Nordea, and DnB Nord) and persuaded them to commit to recapitalization of their subsidiaries there. The four banks declared: "We are committed to meeting the capital and liquidity needs of our subsidiaries and branches in Latvia...."[60] In February 2010, this agreement was renewed between the foreign banks.

When the crisis abated in September 2009, the government drew the following lessons from the crisis:

1. Reforms start when the money runs out, and the need for many reforms in the health care and education sectors was already known.

2. There is always a way out of a crisis. In Latvia's case it is the adoption of the euro in 2014, which will provide domestic stability and international credibility.

3. The broad participation of social partners in the most important government decisions is vital.

4. Courageous decisions have to be made without delay.[61]

Budget for 2010

In mid-October 2009, the last devaluation scare occurred. The chief financial officer of Swedbank, apparently referring to the old IMF idea of a devaluation of 15 percent, expressed his view that Latvia could manage such a devaluation. Financial markets reacted negatively to this comment, and the Polish zloty and other east European currencies declined slightly again. This worry, however, lacked substance.[62]

The same month, the IMF and the European Union demanded another round of budget consolidation of 500 million lats or 4.2 percent of GDP for 2010, which brought the last wave of crisis, since the government and the IMF/European Commission disagreed about the 2010 budget consolidation targets. The government insisted that the agreed 2010 budget deficit target of 8.5 percent of GDP (in ESA95 terms) could be reached with an additional adjustment of 325 million lats, whereas the IMF/European Commission pushed for 500 million lats. But the drama soon ebbed. Latvia suffered from the prior setting of double targets, and the international creditors demanded that the most difficult one should be fulfilled, while the budget deficit seemed the most relevant. Given the asymmetric bargaining power, the government eventually had to do more or less what its creditors demanded. From September 2009, interest rates and other financial conditions started normalizing.

The government's prior norms greatly helped it. It repeated its mantra in its 2010 budget report:

> The goals of the program for stabilization of Latvia's economy remain the same—a stable monetary policy based on a fixed peg of the lats to the euro, as

well as tight fiscal policy. The medium-term objective of fiscal consolidation is to reduce the 2012 general government deficit to the level set by the Maastricht criteria—3% of GDP.[63]

The government continued its practice of consulting its social partners, the Employers' Confederation, the Free Trade Union Confederation, the Chamber of Commerce and Industry, and the Association of Local and Regional Governments, as well as the public through the internet. It maintained minimum spending levels for education, health care, the social sector, public order, and security, notably at least 3.4 percent of GDP for health care funding.

In my budget address to the parliament in November 2009, I stayed downbeat: "This is still a crisis budget. Even if there are some signs of improvement of the economic situation, we still have not overcome the crisis. Therefore, I have no illusions and I am aware that no one will be completely satisfied with the budget. This budget reveals the limited opportunities of the state."[64]

The budget deficit for 2010 was set at 7.5 percent of GDP (ESA95 terms) or 1 percent of GDP below the agreed program target. Since it had taken office in March 2009, the government assessed that it had carried out a fiscal consolidation of approximately 1 billion lats, or 7.6 percent of GDP. Including what the previous government had done, Latvia's total fiscal adjustment in 2009 was 9.5 percent of GDP.

Expenditure cuts had already gone so far that the government suggested larger revenue measures (2.3 percent of GDP) than spending measures (1.9 percent of GDP) for 2010. The much appreciated flat personal income tax of 23 percent could no longer be defended and had to hiked to 26 percent, which upset the business community, as both Estonia and Lithuania had a flat income tax of 21 percent. The real estate tax base was broadened to include residential buildings and construction. Capital gains and capital revenue taxes were introduced. Car taxes were increased, and a new tax for the use of the company's car for private purposes was introduced.

At this time, the new government had been in office for almost eight months, and had had some time to prepare structural reforms. The state administration had already been streamlined. The number of state agencies subordinated to the ministries was reduced from 76 at the beginning of 2009 to 25 at the end of year, a reduction by two-thirds. The government also proposed simplification of the civil service, aiming at making it compact, standardized, professional, and politically neutral. The total number of public employees was to be trimmed down to 8 percent of the total workforce by 2013. Yet the government raised the salaries of the teachers to bring them into parity with those of other public employees to improve their incentives.[65] However, even after the rise, teachers' wages were some 20 percent below their 2008 level.

In parallel, the government attempted to reduce bureaucratic obstacles hampering enterprise, making decisions to steadily dismantle administrative burdens. In particular, the government wanted to facilitate the development of micro enterprises by simplifying their accounting and tax payment requirements as well as capital and business registration costs.[66] The parliament adopted the budget on December 1.

However, after the budget for 2010 was adopted, the Latvian Constitutional Court reversed the pension cuts as unconstitutional on December 21, 2009, and ordered the government to refund the pensioners. As a consequence, fiscal cuts of 1 percent of GDP were undone. Given the fact that the adopted 2010 budget deficit was already 1 percent of GDP below the program target of 8.5 percent of GDP, this additional expenditure was accommodated without a need to find alternative belt-tightening.

On New Year's Eve, I reflected on the past year, recognizing what had gone wrong in Latvia in a year of the most profound economic setback:

> The last minutes of the year elapse—the year that has brought serious lessons and unexpected change to Latvia, the year that will become a turning point in the history of our restored state. Each of us has gone through a bitter experience. But we have also learnt to help those who experience even more difficult times. We were put to shame for past mistakes made in the economy.... This year we experienced the most dramatic economic downturn and the highest unemployment rate in the European Union.... Many painful decisions had to be made in the area of health care, education and [the] social sector.....
>
> The previous years' policy—"Top Gear!"—has failed. The story about seven "good years" seems tragicomic. Unfortunately, every single family and enterprise knows the price that we are paying for these mistakes. Both domestic and foreign experts had warned Latvia about the economy overheating and the risk of a hard landing....
>
> During the years of economic growth the governments lived beyond their means and did not accumulate any savings. For example, Estonia...accumulated savings and therefore survived this crisis more easily than Latvia."[67]

Yet, I made one positive observation: "Since spring we have been working to ensure the solvency of the country, and we have succeeded." My closing line was upbeat: "Let us correct the past mistakes and be proud of our country!"[68]

Notes

1. Robert Anderson, "Latvia Capital Gripped by Riots," *Financial Times*, January 15, 2009.

2. DELFI, "Pētījums: Latvijā augstākais neuzticības rādītājs valdībai un parlamentam Eiropā" ["Opinion Poll: Latvians Do Not Trust the Government and the European Parliament"], January 16, 2009, www.delfi.lv; DELFI, "Vairākums vēlētāju atbalsta Saeimas atlaišanu" ["Majority of Voters Supports Dissolution of Saeima"], January 24, 2009, www.delfi.lv.

3. DELFI, "Saeimas ārkārtas vēlēšanas ir politiķu dienas kārtībā" ["Parliamentary Elections on the Political Agenda"], January 16, 2009, www.delfi.lv.

4. DELFI, "Zatlers: Godmanis ir zaudējis manu uzticību" ["Zatlers: Godmanis Has Lost My Trust"], February 13, 2009, www.delfi.lv.

5. Robert Anderson, "Latvia in Turmoil as Premier Resigns," *Financial Times*, February 21, 2009.

6. Lars Christensen, "Latvia: Mr. Dombrovskis Nominated as New PM," Flash Comment, Danske Bank, February 26, 2009, www.danskebank.dk.

7. DELFI, "Mirskyi: Dombrovskis utonet, kak loshadka" ["Mirskyi: Dombrovskis Will Sink Like a Horse"], March 13, 2009, www.delfi.lv.

8. DELFI, "Pressa: Dombrovskis–prem'er-kamikadze" ["The Press: Dombrovskis – Prime Minister Kamikaze"], February 27, 2009, www.delfi.lv.

9. DELFI, "Mirskyi: Dombrovskis utonet, kak loshadka" ["Mirskyi: Dombrovskis Will Sink Like a Horse"].

10. DELFI, "Opros: rastet populyarnost' JL, TsS i ZaPChEL" ["Poll: Growing Popularity for New Era, Harmony Center, and For Human Rights in United Latvia"], March 23, 2009, www.delfi.lv.

11. DELFI, "Ekspert: takogo padeniya VVP ne bylo so vremen Vtoroi mirovoi voiny" ["Expert: Such Drops in GDP Not Seen Since World War II"], February 20, 2009, www.delfi.lv.

12. Kira Savchenko, "Repshe: Latviya ne poluchit sleduyushchego transha" ["Repshe: Latvia Will Not Receive the Next Tranche"], *Biznes & Baltiya*, April 16, 2009.

13. Robert Anderson, "Deficit Causes IMF to Delay Loans to Riga," *Financial Times*, April 3, 2009.

14. Stefan Wagstyl, "Five-Party Coalition Pledges to Tackle Latvia's Economic Crisis," *Financial Times*, March 5, 2009.

15. LETA, "Dombrovskis tomēr plāno 'mehāniski samazināt' izdevumus visām nozarēm par 20%" ["Dombrovskis Plans a Mechanical Reduction of Expenditures for All Sectors by 20%"], March 2, 2009.

16. Cabinet of Ministers of the Republic of Latvia, "Transcript of the Meeting of Prime Minister of the Republic of Latvia Valdis Dombrovskis with the Representatives of the International Mass Media on Monday, March 23, 2009," State Chancellery, March 27, 2009, www.mk.gov.lv (accessed on December 7, 2010).

17. Ibid.

18. Ibid.

19. Ibid.

20. Ibid.

21. Cabinet of Ministers of the Republic of Latvia, "Agreements on Selling Shares of Parex Bank Signed with the European Bank for Reconstruction and Development," April 16, 2009, www.mk.gov.lv (accessed on December 15, 2010).

22. Ibid.

23. DELFI, "Dombrovskis: Legche stanet vo vtoroi polovine 2010 goda" ["Dombrovskis: The Second Half of 2010 Will Be Better"], March 11, 2009.

24. Camilla Anderson, "Latvia Caught in Vicious Economic Downturn," *IMF Survey Online*, International Monetary Fund, May 28, 2009.

25. LETA, "SVF eksperti mudina koalīciju veikt radikālas strukturālas izmaiņas un pārstrādāt valsts budžetu" ["IMF Experts Suggest Radical Structural Changes and Rethinking the Government Budget"], March 30, 2009.

26. DELFI, "Dombrovskis: Bankrota gadījumā jārēķinās ar drastisku taupību" ["Dombrovskis: In Case of Bankruptcy Drastic Measures Will Be Undertaken"], April 8, 2009.

27. Alberto F. Alesina and Silvia Ardagna, "Large Changes in Fiscal Policy: Taxes Versus Spending," NBER Working Paper 15438 (Cambridge: National Bureau of Economic Research, 2009).

28. LETA, "KM urezhet raskhody i provedet strukturnye reformy" ["KM Will Cut Costs and Conduct Structural Reforms"], April 1, 2009.

29. LETA, "Pravitel'stvo gotovit radikal'nuyu ekonomiyu" ["The Government is Preparing a Radical Economy"], April 21, 2009.

30. DELFI, "Dombrovskis pieprasa Eglītim par 44% samazināt veselības aprūpes administrācij ā strādājošo skaitu," ["Dombrovskis Demands that Eglītis Cuts Administrative Expenditures in Healthcare by 44%"], April 24, 2009, www.delfi.lv.

31. DELFI, "V Latvii iz 59 bol'nits ostanetsya tol'ko 24" ["In Latvia Only 24 out of 59 Hospitals Will Remain"], April 24, 2009.

32. World Bank, *Latvia: From Exuberance to Prudence. A Public Expenditure Review of Government Administration and the Social Sectors*, Report no. 56747-LV, volume 2 (Washington: World Bank, September 27, 2010, 156, 159, 167–68).

33. LETA, "Valsts pārvaldē plānots likvidēt 8000 štata vietu" ["Plans to Liquidate 8000 Staff Positions in Public Administration"], May 15, 2009.

34. LETA, "Seim srezal zarplaty v sovetakh gospredpriyatii" ["Seim Cut Salaries of State-Owned Enterprise Boards"], April 30, 2009.

35. LETA, "VID atlaidīs 1200 darbinieku un strādās četras darba dienas" ["SRS Will Fire 1200 Workers and Will Work Four Day Each Week"], May 14, 2009.

36. Because of the practice of paying various one-off end-of-year bonuses in December, that month is better avoided for comparisons.

37. European Commission, "European Cohesion Policy in Latvia: Cohesion Policy 2007–13," 2009, http://ec.europa.eu (accessed on January 22, 2011).

38. LETA, "Šķēle: ieņēmumu samazināšana iedzīvotājiem ir daudz nepatīkamāks ceļš nekā lata devalvācija" ["Šķēle: A Reduction of the Population's Income is Far More Unpleasant than a Devaluation"], March 21, 2009.

39. LETA, "Laikraksts: Šķēle ieinteresēts lata devalvācijā, jo pārņēmis milzīgas parādsaistības latos" ["Šķēle Is Interested in the Devaluation of the Lat After Having Taken Enormous Debts in Lat"], June 5, 2009.

40. Cabinet of Ministers of the Republic of Latvia, "Announcement by Prime Minister Valdis Dombrovskis in Relation to an Opinion Expressed by Bengt Dennis, Member of the High Level Advisors Group to the Government of Latvia, about Devaluation of the Latvian Currency," State Chancellery, June 2, 2009, www.mk.gov.lv (accessed on December 7, 2010).

41. Nouriel Roubini, "Latvia's Currency Crisis Is a Rerun of Argentina's," *Financial Times*, June 11, 2009, 9.

42. Niklas Magnusson, "Rogoff Says Latvia Should Devalue Its Currency," Bloomberg, June 29, 2009.

43. Central Election Commission, "Local Elections 2009," web.cvk.lv/pub/public/29487.html (accessed on January 1, 2011).

44. Central Election Commission, "Elections to the European Parliament 2009," web.cvk.lv/pub/public/29439.html (accessed on January 1, 2011).

45. Cabinet of Ministers of the Republic of Latvia, "Address by Prime Minister Valdis Dombrovskis at the Extraordinary Session of the Saeima on the 2009 Budget Amendments on 4 June 2009," State Chancellery, June 4, 2009, www.mk.gov.lv (accessed on December 15, 2010).

46. Cabinet of Ministers of the Republic of Latvia, "Government Will Continue Work on Budget Amendments after Their Submission to the Saeima," State Chancellery, June 2, 2009. www.mk.gov.lv (accessed on December 7, 2010).

47. Cabinet of Ministers of the Republic of Latvia, "Full Transcript of the Meeting of Prime Minister of Latvia Valdis Dombrovskis with the Representatives of the International Mass Media on May 14, 2009," State Chancellery, May 14, 2009, www.mk.gov.lv (accessed on December 7, 2010).

48. Cabinet of Ministers of the Republic of Latvia, "Government Will Continue Work on Budget Amendments."

49. Cabinet of Ministers of the Republic of Latvia, "Interview: Latvia Has Succeeded in Persuading Its International Partners Not to Request an Additional VAT Increase," State Chancellery, June 4, 2009, www.mk.gov.lv (accessed on December 7, 2010).

50. Cabinet of Ministers of the Republic of Latvia, "Full Transcript of the Meeting of Prime Minister of Latvia Valdis Dombrovskis with the Representatives of the International Mass Media on May 14, 2009."

51. Cabinet of Ministers of the Republic of Latvia, "Interview: Latvia Has Succeeded in Persuading Its International Partners Not to Request an Additional VAT Increase."

52. Cabinet of Ministers of the Republic of Latvia, "The Information Disseminated to the Mass Media that the Latvian Government Headed by Prime Minister Valdis Dombrovskis Is about to Resign Is False and Deceptive," State Chancellery, June 11, 2009, www.mk.gov.lv (accessed on December 15, 2010).

53. Cabinet of Ministers of the Republic of Latvia, "Agreement of the Government and Social Partners on a 2009 Budget Deficit Reduction in the Amount of 500 Million LVL," State Chancellery, June 12, 2009, www.mk.gov.lv (accessed on December 15, 2010).

54. European Commission, "Cross-Country Study: Economic Policy Changes in the Baltics," *European Economy*, Occasional Papers 58 (Brussels: European Commission, February 2010, 68).

55. Information from the Bank of Latvia website.

56. International Monetary Fund, Republic of Latvia, "Third Review under the Stand-By Arrangement and Financing Assurances Review," July 6, 2010, 10, www.imf.org.

57. Cabinet of Ministers of the Republic of Latvia, "Heads of the EU Member States Express Strong Support for Further Allocation of International Aid for Latvia," www.mk.gov.lv (accessed on December 15, 2010).

58. Edward Hugh, "Are the IMF and the ECB Lining up Against the EU Commission over Latvia?" RGE Monitor, June 30, 2009.

59. International Monetary Fund, "IMF Reaches Staff-level Agreement with the Latvian Authorities on First Review under Stand-by Arrangement," press release, July 27, 2009.

60. Hugh, "Are the IMF and the ECB Lining up Against the EU Commission over Latvia?"

61. "Concluding Statement by Participating Parent Banks," European Banking Group Coordination Meeting for Latvia, Stockholm, Sweden, September 11, 2009, www.imf.org. Such programs were also adopted for Bosnia, Hungary, Romania, Serbia, and Ukraine ("European Bank Coordination Meeting: International Coordination Helped Avert a Systemic Bank Crisis in Central and Eastern Europe," press release, Brussels, September 25, 2009.)

62. Cabinet of Ministers of the Republic of Latvia, "The Prime Minister Emphasizes Latvia's Experience Gained in Coping with the Economic Crisis," State Chancellery, September 24, 2009, www.mk.gov.lv (accessed on December 15, 2010).

63. Piotr Skolimowski, "Zloty Falls as Swedbank Says Latvia Could Manage Devaluation," Bloomberg, October 16, 2009.

64. Cabinet of Ministers of the Republic of Latvia, "V. Dombrovskis Emphasizes the New and Qualitative Approach to Drafting of the 2010 Budget," State Chancellery, November 2, 2009, www.mk.gov.lv (accessed on December 15, 2010).

65. Cabinet of Ministers of the Republic of Latvia, "Address by Prime Minister Valdis Dombrovskis to the Saeima Members," State Chancellery, November 5, 2009, www.mk.gov.lv (accessed on December 15, 2010).

66. Ibid., 12.

67. Ibid.

68. Cabinet of Ministers of the Republic of Latvia, "Address by Prime Minister Valdis Dombrovskis on December 31, 2009," State Chancellery, January 6, 2010, www.mk.gov.lv (accessed on December 15, 2010).

69. Ibid.

6

The Healing Begins, 2010

As the New Year bells rang in 2010, Latvia started rising from the ashes of its deep economic recession. Exports and manufacturing recovered with refreshing vigor, and the ever worse news of the first half of 2009 was replaced with an ever brightening outlook.

For Latvia, it was of great importance that in the spring of 2010 Estonia qualified for the adoption of the euro on January 1, 2011, because this meant that the European Union and the European Central Bank (ECB) accepted to expand the Economic and Monetary Union (EMU) and it signaled the end of the Baltic financial crisis. For Europe as a whole, however, the Greek financial crisis that came to a head in the first days of May 2010 and the broader euro crisis dominated. These crises were followed by eruptions in Ireland, Portugal, and Spain, making Latvia's economy look calm and well-managed. Suddenly, its internal devaluation stood out as a viable strategy for euro area countries in dire financial straits.

The big Latvian event in 2010 was the parliamentary elections in October, which resulted in the victory of the incumbent government. The People's Party had defected from the government in March 2010, for which the voters punished it. A month after the elections, I formed government for the second time consisting of only two political blocs with a majority of their own, replacing the four-party minority government.

In the third quarter of 2010, Latvia finally returned to economic growth after nine quarters of declining output. With steadily improving economic forecasts the government could trim the planned austerity measures. The financial crisis was over, but its effects will linger for years.

Estonia Qualifies for the Euro, March–June 2010

In spite of the global financial crisis, Estonia quietly pursued its accession to the EMU. On May 12, 2010, the European Commission published its annual Convergence Report. After noticing that Estonia met the criteria on price stability, budget balance, public debt, and exchange rate stability, the Commission concluded that Estonia had complied with the convergence criteria and "that Estonia fulfils the conditions for the adoption of the euro."[1] On July 13, the EU finance ministers made the final decision and decided to keep the existing exchange rate to the euro. On January 1, 2011, Estonia introduced the euro without any problem.

Estonia is a stark example for other countries with currency boards. On the one hand, it had shown that it is possible to comply with the Maastricht criteria in the midst of financial crisis. On the other hand, it had also shown the danger of inflation. Although Estonia did not devalue and went through a severe recession, its inflation year over year had reached 5.1 percent in November 2010, and annualized GDP growth was no less than 5 percent in the third quarter of 2010. Clearly, the main threat was not recession or deflation but inflation. In that case, devaluation made no sense.

The governments of Bulgaria, Lithuania, and Latvia were keenly aware of the Estonian experience and welcomed Estonia's entry into the eurozone. They are all determined to achieve a budget deficit of no more than 3 percent of GDP in 2012 in order to be allowed to adopt the euro in 2014. Estonia's entry showed that the door to the eurozone is still open.

Beginning in March 2010, when Estonia's EMU accession appeared likely, the three big rating agencies started raising first the outlook and eventually the ratings for the three Baltic states "on faster-than-anticipated rebounds." Moody's analyst for the Baltic countries commented on Latvia: "The prospect of a disorderly currency devaluation is now highly unlikely."[2]

The Greek financial crisis in April–May 2010 did not harm Latvia. On the contrary, it offered the country an opportunity to shine as a bold and successful pioneer. The Latvian example showed that devaluation was not necessary. A European democracy and welfare state could carry out an internal devaluation, slashing its budget deficit by more than one-tenth of GDP mainly by cutting public expenditures. "The Greek situation is similar to Latvia's in that there is no other choice but to downsize expenditures," Bank of Latvia Governor Ilmārs Rimšēvičs commented to Bloomberg. "We are very pleased that Latvia is more and more mentioned as a template because a year ago people were thinking we [were] going to fail. Today, [Latvia is] more or less out of the woods."[3]

October 2010 Parliamentary Elections: Popular Approval of Crisis Resolution

On October 2, 2010, Latvia held ordinary parliamentary elections. The dominating theme was crisis resolution after a total output fall of 25 percent and unemployment of 20 percent. The surprising outcome was an overwhelming victory for the incumbent government.

Positioning itself for the October parliamentary elections, the People's Party departed from the government coalition in March 2010, distancing itself from the austerity policy. Its leader, Andris Šķēle, had persistently advocated devaluation. With ordinary elections half a year away, it made little sense for the government to resign. It continued ruling with minority support in parliament, but legislation came to a near halt.

In May 2010, the government decided to divide Parex Bank into two banks, a "bad bank" for nonperforming loans and a normal bank. The bad bank was supposed to sell off impaired assets at a deliberate speed to receive decent returns for the state and then be closed down, while the good Parex Bank, renamed Citadele, was to be sold. Sweden had used this technique during its banking crisis in the early 1990s. The plan faced strong objections from the opposition, however, mainly Harmony Center and People's Party. They tried to halt the plan through legislative proposals, apparently to reward the two former owners of Parex Bank, but they never gathered a majority. In May the opposition tried to oust New Era Minister of Interior Linda Mūrniece in a vote of no confidence and in early June to oust New Era Minister of Economy Artis Kampars in repeated votes of no confidence, but these efforts failed.

The elections were preceded by a consolidation of the political parties. On the center-right, New Era gathered Civic Union and Society for Different Politics, forming a political bloc called Unity. On the oligarchic right, Šķēle and Ainārs Šlesers merged their two parties (Latvia's First Party/Latvia's Way and People's Party) into the new business bloc For a Good Latvia, which opposed the government. On the Russian side, Harmony Center became all dominant, persistently the biggest party in opinion polls. The permanent government party, Union of Greens and Farmers, kept a low profile but maintained its high popularity. Apart from two small Latvian and Russian nationalistic parties, the political stage had consolidated.

The election campaign became a battle between the three leading candidates for prime minister: Jānis Urbanovičs of Harmony Center, Šlesers of For a Good Latvia, and myself. The economic crisis and the International Monetary Fund (IMF)/European Union program dominated the debate. For a Good Latvia and Harmony Center criticized the government's austerity policy, the IMF, and the Swedish banks in a pretty populist fashion, claiming that the cost had been much higher than necessary and advocating lower public cuts and devaluation. A typical Šlesers statement was: "The government should not have to bow to the IMF...."[4] They also claimed that a vote for me was really a vote for Lembergs, whose Union of Greens and Farmers would clearly be part of a new government led by New Era.

Unity advocated a clean and small government, fiscal discipline, and export-oriented recovery. Its advocacy can be summarized in one phrase: "We are on the right road." On August 9, I claimed: "The recession is over and... it can be expected that in the second [half] of the year Latvia's economy will regain growth...[of] gross domestic product, tax income, employment...."[5] Unity insisted that nobody could have taken the country out of the crisis at a smaller cost. It acknowledged the severity of the crisis but blamed its oligarchic predecessors.

On October 2, Latvians offered a resounding vote of confidence in the incumbent center-right minority government. The big winner was Unity, which received 31.2 percent of the votes and 33 seats in parliament. Its main coalition partner, the Union of Greens and Farmers, obtained 19.7 percent of the votes and 22 seats (table 6.1). Together, these two parties held a majority.

Harmony Center increased its votes substantially from 14.4 percent in 2006 to 26.0 percent. Like New Era, Harmony Center had benefited from being in the opposition to the government that had led Latvia into the crisis. But then it criticized the policies of the succeeding, anticrisis government, favoring a much larger budget deficit and toying with devaluation. Its rating slumped during its populist preelection campaign.

Most of all, oligarchic populism suffered a devastating blow. The big loser was For a Good Latvia, with Šlesers and Šķēle. Because of poor poll numbers they had merged their two parties to stay in parliament, but even so their combined votes plunged from 28.2 percent in 2006 to 7.7 percent. Even the superior campaign financing and media access of For a Good Latvia and Harmony Center did not help. One reason may have been that the internet played an increasingly significant role in the Latvian news room.

These elections appear to be a textbook example of how a serious and competent government can win elections even with severe austerity policy, if it convinces the voters.[6] My assessment of the outcome was: "Voters have sent a quite clear message that they prefer stability and continuity."[7] Populism was no longer very popular in this part of the world, while economic rationality was. Ultimately, the incumbent government appeared more credible as an economic manager. The elections confirmed that Latvia had worked itself out of its severe economic crisis. Its IMF/European Union program had proven not only an economic success but also a political one. Devaluation was neither necessary nor inevitable. Internal devaluation was a viable policy and politically more popular.

For outside observers, the government's victory was quite a surprise. It was "good news for Latvia and good news for the economy," Lars Christensen of Danske Bank commented.[8] Yarkin Cebeci of JPMorgan Chase & Co. noted: "Thanks to the rigorous implementation of the economic program Latvia escaped a devaluation whose repercussions could have been much more serious."[9]

The sitting coalition government increased its majority in parliament from 45 to 63 seats. The natural conclusion was that it would continue to rule, as the Latvian people had clearly approved of its austerity program, the fixed exchange rate, and the IMF/European Union cooperation, but a reconfiguration was considered. For a Good Latvia was out of question, having pursued a populist campaign against the government's policy and been roundly beaten.

Table 6.1   Results of the parliamentary elections, 2006 and 2010

	2006			2010	
Party	Percent of votes	Seats	Party	Percent of votes	Seats
People's Party	19.6	23	For a Good Latvia[a]	7.7	8
Latvia's First Party/Latvia's Way	8.6	10		n.a.	n.a.
Union of Greens and Farmers	16.7	18		19.7	22
For Fatherland and Freedom	6.9	8		7.7	8
New Era	16.4	18	Unity[b]	31.2	33
Harmony Center	14.4	17		26.0	29
For Human Rights in United Latvia	6.0	6		1.4	0
Other parties	10.0	0		6.0	0
Total	100.0	100		100.0	100

n.a. = not applicable

a. In 2010, People's Party and Latvia's First Party/Latvia's Way merged into For a Good Latvia.
b. In 2010, New Era formed a political bloc called Unity with Civic Union and Society for Different Politics.

Source: Central Election Commission of Latvia, www.cvk.lv (accessed on November 30, 2010).

Harmony Center had also pursued a populist campaign, but it had gained greatly. Unity invited Harmony Center to join the government on certain conditions. Harmony Center had to recognize that Latvia had been occupied by the Soviet Union during World War II, that Latvian would stay the single state language, and that the West-oriented foreign policy would be maintained. However, Harmony Center protested against these conditions and was not prepared to recognize that Latvia had been occupied. It also voted against Latvia's continued military participation in Afghanistan, excluding itself from government once again. The Society for Different Politics, one of the two partners of New Era in the Unity bloc, vetoed the participation of All for Latvia!/For Fatherland and Freedom/Latvian National Independence movement for being too nationalistic.

As a consequence, I continued as prime minister in a two-bloc coalition consisting of Unity and the Union of Greens and Farmers, the eternal government party, with a solid majority of 55 seats. President Valdis Zatlers nominated me as prime minister exactly one month after the elections, and on November 3 the parliament voted 63-35 for the coalition. This was a small government with only 14 ministers, eight from Unity and six from the Union of Greens and Farmers. Unity took care of the economy, foreign affairs, defense, and justice, while all the social portfolios, agriculture, environment, and regional development went to the Greens and Farmers. Finance Minister Einars Repše had declared early on that he wanted to leave politics. His place was filled by Andris Vilks, who had been the Swedish bank SEB's chief economist in Latvia.

Incidentally, Latvia's relations with Russia improved following the financial crisis. Bilateral problems have been gradually sorted out or eliminated. The border dispute was settled in March 2007. Moscow impressed Riga by not trying to exploit Latvia's financial crisis and the January 2009 riots. In December 2010, President Zatlers was invited to Russia for an official presidential visit. Latvia's relations with Russia had become better than ever since Latvia's independence.

Budget for 2011

From the outset of 2010, Latvia seemed to have turned its economy around, and all economic statistics were better than anticipated. As a consequence of the faster than expected recovery in 2010, and thus higher tax revenues, the Latvian government argued that it no longer needed as large cuts in 2011 as had previously been planned.

The budget deficit for 2010 had been planned at 8.5 percent of GDP, and preliminarily it ended up just below that number in European System of Accounts of 1995 (ESA95) terms and around 6.4 percent of GDP in cash terms. For 2011, the government adopted a budget with a deficit of 5.4 percent of GDP (ESA95 terms), which was slightly less than the target of 6 percent of GDP agreed with the IMF and the European Union. On December 20 the parliament passed the 2011 budget with a further fiscal tightening of 2.2 percent of GDP.

In the 2011 budget, taxes accounted for two-thirds of the fiscal adjustment, notably a value-added tax (VAT) hike from 21 to 22 percent, and the reduced VAT rate was increased from 10 to 12 percent, while the real estate tax for residential buildings was doubled. Yet, the flat personal income tax was cut from 26 to 25 percent and the personal exemption increased, but the social security contribution rate was increased from 33 to 35 percent of the payroll. The car tax was made more progressive, being reduced for smaller cars and increased for bigger cars. In addition, the minimum wage was raised from 180 lats a month to 200 lats a month, which the government saw as a way of reducing the shadow economy, where higher wages than declared are paid.[10]

But the IMF and European Commission missions disagreed with the government about how large the fiscal adjustment really was. A joint IMF/European Commission team that visited Riga December 7–14 called for "additional high-quality structural measures of at least LVL 50 million" (0.4 percent of GDP) in 2011 "to bring down the general government deficit below the program's 2011 ceiling of 6 percent of GDP." The joint team admonished the Latvian government to keep "the 2012 general government deficit significantly below 3 percent of GDP," taking a harder stand than previously.[11]

An outside observer gets the impression that the IMF and the European Commission wanted to overinsure themselves, while the Latvian government saw the strong rebound in the economy and tax revenues and did not want to impose more hardship on already suffering Latvians than really necessary. The difference was not one of principle but of assessment of economic development and incentives.

In addition, the European Union also requested that the Latvian government prepare a list of state companies slated for privatization. But the government opposed early privatization, seeing it as a firesale. It preferred to wait for better prices as the economy recovered. This was a typical dispute between a creditor desiring early asset sales to secure repayment and a debtor hoping for higher prices in the future. Moreover, privatization was politically sensitive because during the election campaign Šlesers had claimed that the government had concluded a secret agreement with the international donors about large-scale privatization immediately after the elections.[12]

The Latvian government was in a new and more favorable position, as the financial crisis that had erupted in late 2007 was effectively over. Latvia would not necessarily need more of the committed international financial support. It had received €4.4 billion or 58 percent of the €7.5 billion international credit package. The €2.2 billion from the Nordic countries, Czech Republic, and Poland was left untouched (table 3.2).[13]

The government started issuing two- to three-year treasury bonds in 2010. Finance Minister Andris Vilks anticipated that the Latvian government might return to the international bond market in the second half of 2011 after it received one more credit rating upgrade. Moody's maintained Latvia at investment grade, while Standard & Poor's upgraded it. Both Standard & Poor's and Fitch Ratings kept Latvia one notch below investment rating. Vilks wanted one of these two agencies to raise the rating to investment grade. On March 15, 2011, Fitch Ratings raised Latvia to investment grade. The yield on Latvia's 5.5 percent bond due in March 2018 had peaked at 12 percent in March 2008. In late 2010, it traded at a yield of 5.2 to 5.3 percent, which was less than what bilateral government loans would have cost.[14] In February 2011, Latvia held an auction for ten-year bonds in lats, and the whole volume on offer of $20 million was sold at an average interest of 6.72 percent.

Still, Latvia's financial situation remained precarious. The economic branch of the government was in a tight spot. On the one hand, its coalition partner, the Union of Greens and Farmers, opposed all further fiscal adjustment. On the other hand, the European Union and the IMF were as tough as ever. In February 2011, the New Era ministers finally managed to persuade coalition partners to adopt a supplementary budget to satisfy the demands of the European Union and the IMF, reducing the expected budget deficit to 5 percent of GDP. Interestingly, it was more politically difficult to adopt this fiscal adjustment of 0.4 percent of GDP than it had been to promulgate the belt-tightening of 11 percent of GDP in 2009.

In the midst of the crisis, apprehension had arisen on the basis of IMF calculations that Latvia's public debt would rise to 90 percent of GDP. At the end of 2010, however, it was a moderate 42 percent of GDP, and the somewhat pessimistic IMF forecast was that it would peak at 50 percent of GDP, well below the Maastricht public debt target of 60 percent of GDP. Instead, inflation had become the main Latvian concern as before the crisis. By December 2010, annualized consumer price inflation had already reached 2.5 percent a year, and in January 2011 it surged to 3.7 percent with the VAT hike.[15]

Economic Growth Returns

Latvia went through a dramatic crisis and turnaround in the three years 2008 to 2010. Economic policy during this period was multifaceted. The immediate concern was to restore financial stability. In doing so, the government also aimed at improving economic competitiveness and efficiency of public services. Substantial advances were made, and after two years economic growth returned.

The nation had suffered an abysmal period of nine consecutive quarters of declining GDP in annualized terms from the second quarter of 2008 through the second quarter of 2010. The total fall in GDP was 25 percent. The darkest period was 2009, when GDP plunged by 18 percent. Unemployment peaked at 20.7 percent in early 2010 (figure 5.4). The driving disaster was the real estate crisis, where prices plunged by 70 percent in two years from a sharp peak in early 2007 until early 2009.[16]

The causes of Latvia's crisis were entirely financial. There was no supply or demand shock or terms-of-trade change. The underlying cause was that Latvia lived on excessive short-term bank borrowing, and the crisis became severe because of a sudden stop of these inflows.

The immediate cause of the economic decline was not lack of external demand but collapse in domestic demand, which could no longer be financed. In 2009 consumption plummeted by 22.4 percent and gross fixed investment by 37.7 percent, driving the decline. Although exports were contracting, net exports surprisingly made a positive contribution to GDP in 2009 because the share of exports in GDP stayed constant, while imports fell by 20 percent more than exports (table 6.2). Gross capital formation or investment halved from 40.4 percent of GDP in 2007 to a still rather high 19 percent of GDP in 2009. The dominant cause of the contraction was that gross national savings skyrocketed from 20 percent of GDP in 2008 to 30.8 percent in 2009. Therefore, the discrepancy between investment and savings became rather extreme at 11.8 percent of GDP (table 6.3).[17]

This increase in savings was not quite voluntary but prompted by the international liquidity cutoff. The Bank of Latvia could not expand the money supply much without risking the country's financial stability. Latvians blamed the Swedish banks for drastically reducing their lending, but these banks were also squeezed. The financial institution that could have provided liquidity was the ECB, but it did not do anything for Latvia or the other Baltic countries. Only in June 2009 was the Swedish Riksbank allowed to borrow a limited amount of €3 billion from the ECB.[18]

In 2010, however, economic recovery in Latvia gathered steam. The economy performed better than forecast each quarter, as GDP swung from a

Table 6.2 Development of aggregate demand, 2007–09
(percent change)

Component	2007	2008	2009
Real GDP	10.0	−4.6	−18.0
Private consumption	14.8	−5.5	−22.4
Public consumption	3.7	1.5	−9.2
Gross fixed investment	7.5	−15.6	−37.7
Exports of goods and services	10.0	−1.3	−13.9
Imports of goods and services	14.7	−13.6	−34.2

Source: International Monetary Fund, Republic of Latvia, "Third Review under the Stand-By Arrangement and Financing Assurances Review," July 6, 2010, 24, www.imf.org.

Table 6.3 Savings and investment, 2007–09 (percent of GDP)

Component	2007	2008	2009
Gross national savings	20.0	20.0	30.8
Gross capital formation	40.4	31.5	19.0
Private investment	34.9	26.4	15.2

Source: International Monetary Fund, Republic of Latvia, "Third Review under the Stand-By Arrangement and Financing Assurances Review," July 6, 2010, 24, www.imf.org.

decline of 16.8 percent in the fourth quarter of 2009 to growth of 2.9 percent in the third quarter of 2010 and 3.7 percent in the fourth quarter (figure 6.1). As 2010 started, the average forecast had been a decline in economic output of 3.5 to 4 percent in 2010, but the preliminary GDP decline was minimal at 0.2 percent.[19] As is usually the case when a small, open economy escapes a recession, early positive results were first recorded in foreign trade and finance, the bellwethers of change. The first and most remarkable turnaround came in foreign trade.

The economic recovery was led by a sudden burst of exports, which rose by 29.5 percent in 2010, dismissing the claim that Latvia did not have much to export. From the start of the crisis in 2008, exports had outperformed imports (figure 6.2). As a consequence, Latvia recorded a current account surplus from the beginning of 2009, which it had not experienced since independence. It turned into a substantial surplus of 9.4 percent of GDP in 2009, and it stayed positive in 2010 (figure 6.3).

The small manufacturing sector drove Latvia's export surge, indicating that the structure of the economy had changed to become more sustainable. Construction, housing, and finance remained depressed, while manufacturing expanded by 14 percent in 2010.[20] Increased export demand for Latvia's wood and metal products were the engines of recovery, but household consumption

Figure 6.1   Quarterly change in GDP, 2007–10

percent of corresponding period of previous year

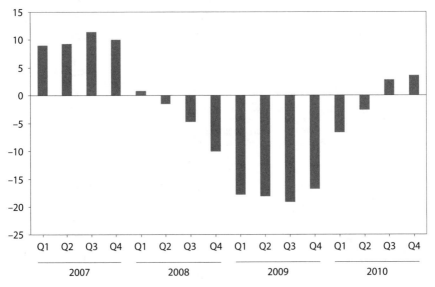

Source: Central Statistical Bureau of Latvia,www.csb.gov.lv (accessed on March 11, 2011).

also contributed.[21] Yet, manufacturing output remains far below the level of 2008 and will need to expand further.

Financial-market conditions have stabilized but are still far from normal. Bank deposits have recovered to precrisis levels, but lending is still falling. Provisioning remains high, and the banks continue to pile up losses. The banks have responded with recapitalization, which has led to continued deleveraging. Latvian banks recorded a total capital-asset ratio of no less than 14 percent, which means that the banks are ready to expand their lending when they find solvent borrowers. The government had to deal with a new banking problem in 2010, when the state-owned, substantially loss-laden Mortgage and Land Bank (MLB) required state recapitalization of 0.6 percent of GDP despite two capital increases in 2009.[22] As for the foreign banks, none left Latvia. Also reassuring are Latvia's international reserves, which have been steadily replenished since July 2009, thanks to generous international financial assistance, in particular the large EU disbursements (figure 5.5). The Bank of Latvia has pursued almost no net foreign exchange intervention since the fall of 2009.

Of the €7.5 billion that was mobilized in international credits for Latvia, the country has used only €4.4 billion, that is, €3.1 billion less than the international community feared would be needed. There are three major explanations why larger funds were not needed. The bulk of the savings arose from

Figure 6.2 Monthly export and import dynamics, 2008–10

percent of corresponding period of previous year

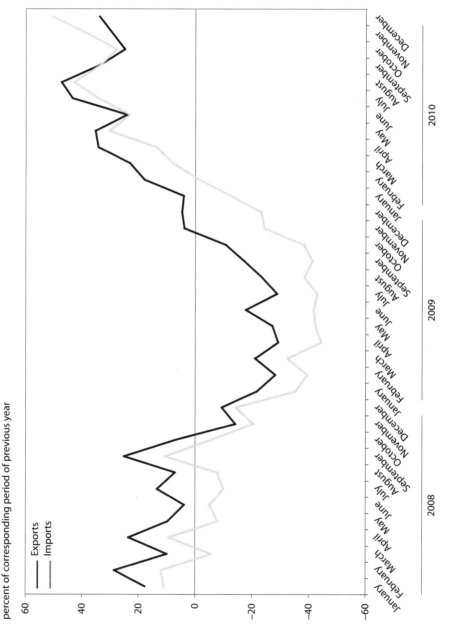

Source: Central Statistical Bureau of Latvia, www.csb.gov.lv (accessed on March 7, 2011).

Figure 6.3   Quarterly current account balance, 2000–10

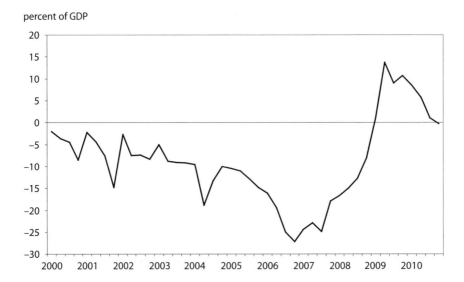

percent of GDP

Source: Bank of Latvia, www.bank.lv (accessed on March 11, 2011).

the banking crisis being much milder than anticipated, essentially stopping at Parex Bank. The banking crisis required barely 5 percent of the 2008 GDP in the course of 2008-09,[23] while 15 to 20 percent of GDP was feared. The Bank of Latvia hopes that the eventual cost of Parex will be only 2 percent of GDP.[24] The government had set aside €2.7 billion of the international assistance package for bank financing, but only €800 million was needed for Parex Bank, that is, a saving of no less than €1.9 billion, largely due to the absence of currency depreciation. The foreign private banks absorbed substantial losses and recapitalized as necessary at their home bases. The second reason was that the Latvian population refrained from any bank or currency run after 2008. Finally, the early radical crisis resolution helped to avoid unpleasant surprises after June 2009.

Latvia's fiscal adjustment was unusually large, and assessments of the fiscal consolidation have been quite similar. The World Bank has produced a reasonable estimate of a total of 13.3 percent of GDP from 2008 to 2010, of which 10.4 percent of GDP was expenditure cuts and 2.8 percent of GDP increased revenue (table 6.4). The Latvian Ministry of Finance puts the same number at 14.1 percent of GDP and for 2011 adds an adjustment of 2.2 percent of GDP to a total of 16.3 percent of GDP (figure 6.4).

Latvia produced four packages of fiscal adjustment: December 2008, June 2009, November 2009, and December 2010. Most of the adjustment was concentrated in 2009. Formally, the adjustment was supposed to be 11 percent

Table 6.4 Fiscal adjustment from 2008 to 2010 (percent of GDP)

Component	2008	2010		
	Actual	Baseline	Projection	Measures
Total revenue	35.2	36.8	39.6	2.8
Total expenditure	38.5	58.2	47.8	10.4
Fiscal balance	−3.3	−21.4	−8.1	13.3

Source: World Bank, "Latvia: From Exuberance to Prudence. A Public Expenditure Review of Government Administration and the Social Sectors," Report no. 56747-LV, volume 2, September 27, 2010, 21.

Figure 6.4   Fiscal consolidation, 2008–11

percent of GDP

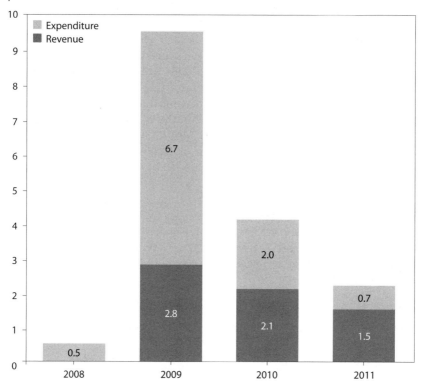

Source: Ministry of Finance of Latvia, Presentation for Meeting of Finance Ministers of Estonia, Latvia and Lithuania, Riga, January 11, 2011.

of GDP in 2009, though the final effect was 9.5 percent of GDP, as many measures were undertaken in the middle of the year (figure 6.4). Ironically, the politically most difficult adjustment package has been the one of December 2010, because then the country was caught in adjustment fatigue. It was much easier to carry out the fiscal tightening early on when the nation faced a clear and real danger.

The fiscal measures carried out in 2009 contained approximately three-quarters expenditure cuts, which was then much easier to implement than revenue measures. Even so, public expenditures rose from 38.5 percent of GDP in 2008 to a forecast 47.8 percent of GDP in 2010 (table 6.4) because of contracting GDP, but this level is likely to fall with economic recovery. Our conclusion is that Latvia was lucky to have pushed so hard for spending reduction in 2009. The Latvian experience illustrates three ideas: that substantial budget deficit cuts are possible in a democracy when necessary, that it is vital to act radically early on, and that it is much easier and more sensible to do the fiscal adjustment through expenditure cuts than through tax increases.

The austerity drive facilitated significant structural reforms that had been desirable for a long time. The most popular was reform of public administration, including the abolition of half of the state agencies and the reduction of civil servants by 30 percent from early 2008 until the third quarter of 2010 (figure 5.2). This downsizing of a state administration must have been one of the biggest during peacetime, and it was accompanied with substantial deregulation. Latvia was already highly ranked on the World Bank Doing Business Index, but it rose from 29th in 2009 to 24th in 2011. The main reason for advancing on the index were improvements in facilitation of closing a business and of registering property.[25]

The public health care and education systems went through badly needed rationalization. The World Bank passed the judgment: "Latvia has achieved years' worth of difficult structural reforms in the short space of just a few months." There was "clear evidence of a shift in health spending, which favors more intensive use of preventive and day-care procedures" and the "heavy burden on the budget of over-capacity of schools and teachers has been lightened significantly."[26]

On the one hand, school directors and local authorities were allowed to be flexible in managing education. On the other, they were offered incentives to improve both efficiency and quality through budget financing based on the number of students attending rather than inputs (schools and teachers). As a consequence, the number of schools was reduced from 992 in 2007–08 to 877 in 2009–10, that is, 115 schools or 12 percent of all schools were closed. The total number of school staff declined in one year, from 2008 to 2009, by 4,000 people or 14 percent. Yet, government spending on education rose from 4.4 percent of GDP in 2008 to 5.1 percent of GDP in 2009, and teachers received a large salary hike in early 2010.[27]

Health care reform was more complex and less radical, but its aim was the same: more efficiency and higher quality. Public employment in health care fell by 2,700 people, or 8 percent, in 2008–09.[28] These public-sector reforms are almost certain to raise national productivity.

The average public wage fell by 26 percent in nominal terms from November 2008 to November 2009, approximately as legislated, while private wages fell much less (figure 5.3). Unit labor costs in manufacturing declined by 21 percent from mid-2008 until end-2009. As a consequence, private employment fell more steeply by at most 33 percent in annualized terms in 2009.[29]

In this deflationary environment, inflation decreased much faster than had been forecast, whereas the deflationary cycle that pessimists had predicted never materialized. The deepest price fall occurred in the first quarter of 2010, when annualized deflation was 3.7 percent (figure 2.4), but it did not last. By the end of 2010, Latvia had annualized inflation of 2.5 percent, showing that the threat of inflation remains potent, though average deflation in 2010 over 2009 was 1.1 percent.

The government parties' agreement with its social partners in June 2009, in the midst of the devaluation scare, proved fortuitous. The government has paid great attention to the social welfare of weak social groups. It has emphasized the need for social equity and peace, and the population seems to have taken this message seriously.

However, the biggest shortcoming of the government's crisis policy has probably been its inability to pursue pension reform. Pension expenditures have been large and retirement age low, with many categories receiving early retirement but low pensions. In the second half of the 1990s, Latvia raised the low Soviet retirement age—60 for men and 55 for women—to an equal 62 years. In 2001, Latvia pioneered a World Bank prototype pension system with three pillars: a public pay-as-you-go minimum pension, a compulsory private saving pension, and private pensions. Gradually, larger pension contributions were supposed to go to compulsory fully funded pensions (the second pillar). By 2008, the share had increased to 8 percent of the income, but it was cut to 2 percent in 2009 to salvage the public pension funding, and it has stayed at that level until 2011.[30] Pension reform has to be restarted in the future.

The government tried to cut pensions by 10 percent in June 2009, but the Constitutional Court reversed that decision and ordered the government to refund withheld pensions in full. Because of the large output contraction and freezing of pensions, the pensions' share of GDP rose during the crisis. Moreover, from 2005 to 2009, the average pension for new retirees increased by 69 percent.[31] Similarly, pension reform has been stalled because of a conflict between building up private mandatory pension funds based on savings and the financing of public pensions, which have won out in the crisis.

In the second half of 2010, Latvia had returned to sound economic growth, and the crisis had abated. The current account was in surplus, and manufacturing exports were rising. The regrettably high unemployment was falling steadily. The bank system had survived and was well capitalized. Latvia may make use of some more international financial support, but the need is no longer urgent. From the spring of 2009, the government had been determined to attempt to adopt the euro in 2014, and this determination stays and appears realistic. Ironically, the main concern has once again become inflation, which reached an annualized rate of 3.7 percent in January 2011, showing that a devaluation was never justified.

Notes

1. European Commission, "Convergence Report 2010," *European Economy*, no. 3 (2010, provisional edition, 11–14).

2. Milda Seputyte, "Baltic Rating Outlooks Raised by Moody's on Recovery," Bloomberg, March 31, 2010.

3. Agnes Lovasz, "Greece Must Copy Baltic Debt Crisis Model to Survive, Finance Chiefs Say," Bloomberg, April 23, 2010.

4. Petr Telegrafov, "Shlezers: pravitel'stvo ne dolzhno klanyat'sya pered MVF" ["Shlezers: The Government Should Not Bow before the IMF"], *Telegraf*, September 30, 2010.

5. Cabinet of Ministers of the Republic of Latvia, "Prime Minister: The Recession Is over, Growth Expected in the Second Half of the Year," State Chancellery, August 9, 2010, www.mk.gov.lv (accessed on December 15, 2010).

6. Aaron Eglitis, "Latvia Ruling Coalition Win Reelection: Dombrovskis Stays Prime Minister," Bloomberg, October 3, 2010.

7. BBC News, "Latvia's ruling centre-right coalition wins elections," October 3, 2010, www.bbc.co.uk.

8. Aaron Eglitis, "Latvia's Dombrovskis Rewarded with Win after Austerity," Bloomberg, October 4, 2010.

9. Ibid.

10. BNS, "Prinyat Byudzhet-2011 s konsolidatsiei v 290 mln latov" ["The 2011 Budget Is Approved with a Consolidation of 290 Million Lats"], December 20, 2010.

11. International Monetary Fund and European Commission, "Joint Statement at the Conclusion of a Staff Visit to Latvia," press release no. 10/495, December 16, 2010.

12. Polina Elksne, "Gospredpriyatiya mogut prodat', chtoby pokryt' mezhdunarodnyi zaem" ["State-Owned Enterprise May Be Sold to Cover International Debt"], *Telegraf*, September 16, 2010, www.telegraf.lv.

13. BNS, "Latvia does not plan to receive further installments of international loan," December 28, 2010.

14. Aaron Eglitis, "Latvian Economy Probably Ended EU's Longest Decline on Increasing Exports," Bloomberg, November 4, 2010; Aaron Eglitis, "Latvia May Return to Eurobond Market Next Year, Finance Chief Vilks Says," Bloomberg, December 17, 2010.

15. BNS, "Inflation in Latvia to Grow Steeper in H1 Than Expected—Finmin," February 8, 2011.

16. Bas B. Bakker and Anne-Marie Gulde, "The Credit Boom in the EU New Member States: Bad Luck or Bad Policies?" IMF Working Paper 10/130, Washington: International Monetary Fund, 2010, 11.

17. Ibid., 24.

18. Riksbanken, "Riksbanken lånar av ECB" ["The Riksbank Borrows from the ECB"], press release, June 10, 2009, www.riksbank.se.

19. "Latvian Q4 GDP Growth Fastest in Three Years," Reuters, February 7, 2011.

20. Central Statistical Bureau of Latvia, Table RU13: Manufacturing Production Output, www.csb.gov.lv (accessed on March 7, 2011).

21. Eglitis, "Latvian Economy Probably Ended EU's Longest Decline on Increasing Exports."

22. International Monetary Fund, Republic of Latvia, "Third Review under the Stand-By Arrangement and Financing Assurances Review," July 6, 2010, 3-4, 10-11, 17, www.imf.org.

23. Ibid., 25.

24. Interview with Governor Rimšēvičs on February 4, 2011.

25. International Finance Corporation/World Bank, Doing Business, www.doingbusiness.org (accessed on January 7, 2011).

26. World Bank, Latvia: From Exuberance to Prudence, 6-7.

27. Ibid., 156, 159, 167-68.

28. Ibid., 186.

29. International Monetary Fund, Republic of Latvia, "Third Review," 3, 6, 7.

30. European Commission, "Cross-Country Study: Economic Policy Changes in the Baltics," Occasional Papers 58 (Brussels, February 2010).

31. World Bank, Latvia: From Exuberance to Prudence, 9.

7

Latvia's Lessons for Itself and the World

We hope this book has offered some food for thought. There is little defense for the overheating of Latvia's economy, but the way the country navigated and successfully overcame the crisis is where we find lessons for Latvia itself and for the world at large. The big issue was exchange rate policy. We have persistently argued that Latvia was right not to have devalued, and we reiterate this point in the following section. We then distinguish between lessons from the crisis resolution that are unique to Latvia and lessons for the rest of the world. Finally, we consider Latvia's economic goals, adoption of the euro, and European economic convergence.

Why Latvia Was Right Not to Have Devalued

It is now evident that Latvia is not going to devalue. The lat's peg to the euro has held, and economic growth returned to Latvia in the third quarter of 2010. All the Jeremiahs whose only question was when Latvia would devalue have been proven wrong. Since most economists were singing this tune, as we discussed in chapter 4, we revisit the arguments with the benefit of hindsight.

In a severe crisis, a successful policy must have simple and clear goals that everyone understands. Therefore nominal anchors, such as exchange rate pegs, budget balances, or monetary targets, are popular remedies. Throughout the crisis, the Latvian government and the Bank of Latvia had two simple and understandable goals: a fixed exchange rate to the euro and a budget deficit of less than 3 percent of GDP by 2012 to render adoption of the euro in 2014 possible. Admittedly, between November 2008 and May 2009, the year of planned accession to the Economic and Monetary Union (EMU) slipped by three years from 2011 to 2014, but that did not blur this target. The peg offered Latvia the desired stable norm for its crisis resolution.

Figure 7.1 Public debt, 2008–12e

percent of GDP

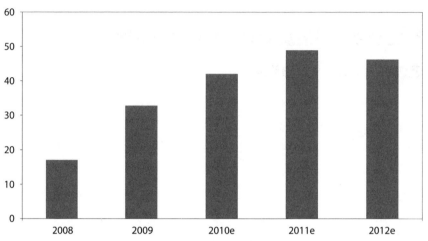

e = estimate

Source: IMF, *World Economic Outlook* database, October 2010, www.imf.org (accessed on November 30, 2010).

A major positive surprise has been that the public cost of bank losses has been far smaller than anticipated. While the International Monetary Fund (IMF) initially expected bank losses amounting to 15 to 20 percent of GDP, they were limited to some 5 percent in 2008–09, essentially the initial cost for the recapitalization of Parex Bank.[1] Moreover, this is a gross cost, much of which may be recovered when the government eventually sells Parex Bank and its assets. Devaluation would have boosted this cost, as more banks would have collapsed and required recapitalization. The government could have escaped such costs, but since Ireland had failed to do so, how likely was Latvia to succeed? As a result, Latvia's public debt remains relatively small at 42 percent of GDP at the end of 2010 (figure 7.1), half of the average public debt of the euro area members. No other plausible policy would have kept the public debt this low.

Gross foreign debt has risen with falling GDP, but it has not doubled, as it would have in the case of devaluation, presumably peaking at 165 percent of GDP in the second quarter of 2010, with net foreign debt at only 58 percent of GDP (figure 7.2). The sustainable level of foreign private debt varies greatly by country, but since foreign creditors refinanced Latvia's debts through this severe crisis, they are likely to continue doing so when economic growth and asset prices recover, and the Latvian government can resume sales of public assets.

Figure 7.2   External debt, 2005–09

percent of GDP

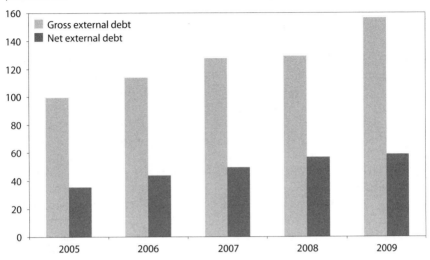

Source: Bank of Latvia, www.bank.lv (accessed on January 5, 2011).

Foreign trade has proven the pessimists more wrong than anything else. Exports rose until September 2008, falling sharply for four months, and then lingered at a low level for seven months before starting a brisk surge in September 2009. By September 2010, exports had fully recovered from their nominal level in September 2008. As imports declined much more steeply, Latvia achieved a current account surplus for the first time in many years in January 2009 (figures 6.2 and 6.3). Manufacturing booms when it is no longer crowded out by housing, construction, finance, and consumption.

The fixed exchange rate forced Latvia to undertake many structural reforms, facilitating higher productivity than would otherwise have been the case. This is a strategic achievement.

The absence of devaluation contributed to social equity and social peace, making policy and social processes more controllable. Undoubtedly, income and wealth differentials increased during the boom years, as is usually the case under inflation. The austerity program, by contrast, explicitly aimed at maintaining social assistance to the poor and pensioners, while cutting salaries of well-to-do senior officials. Devaluation, on the contrary, would primarily have benefited wealthy exporters at the expense of everybody else. Not surprisingly, mainly rich businessmen advocated devaluation.

The ultimate argument against devaluation is that inflation has already become the main concern, having risen to 2.5 percent in December 2010 in spite of the horrendous financial crisis. This shows that devaluation was never justified. Indeed, as advocates of a fixed exchange rate we have argued from the outset that if Latvia had devalued, its adoption of the euro would have stalled for years to come. Latvia's great opportunity to accede to the EMU is in 2014, and then it will never again have to fear being cut off from international liquidity as it was in late 2008 and 2009.

The proponents of devaluation are left with two possible arguments. One is that GDP could have fallen less. Such a proposition appears doubtful, but it is impossible to establish the relevant counterfactual. The liquidity squeeze and the government crisis would have occurred in any case. Devaluation would have broken the Latvian banking system and caused mass bankruptcies because of currency mismatches. Disorderly devaluation would presumably have spread to Lithuania and Estonia, as well as caused a Swedish banking crisis. All the floating exchange rates in the region—the Swedish krona, Polish zloty, Russian ruble, and Czech koruna—would have depreciated significantly. Regional financial chaos reminiscent of the collapse of the European Monetary System in 1992 with cascading devaluations could have erupted with severe repercussions for all concerned.

Moreover, Latvia's problem was not primarily exports, but excessive capital inflows, which suddenly stopped. A comparison with Ukraine may be of some relevance. It devalued by 40 percent in 2008 (mainly because of its falling export prices), but even so it experienced a GDP fall of 15 percent in 2009, while Latvia's decrease was 18 percent. Devaluation would certainly have eased the Latvian GDP decline in the short term, but the risks and social drama would have been far greater. In the long term, however, the structural reforms forced by the stable exchange rate are likely to spur higher growth.

The only strong argument in favor of devaluation is that unemployment might have been lower, because devaluation would have slashed euro wages drastically but thus also the standard of living. Latvia harbors a major concern about emigration, which in all likelihood would have increased after devaluation, because euro wages abroad would have been higher. Emigration did increase in 2009 and more so in 2010, when it reached 0.37 percent, and official statistics may understate emigration, as people do not necessarily register temporary moves. However unfortunate, this is still a limited number but might have been much greater if euro wages had plummeted.

In hindsight, the arguments for the maintenance of the peg appear overwhelming, though not altogether conclusive. In November 2009, one of us (Dombrovskis) summed up his view of devaluation:

> Devaluation would be a non-selective reduction of the real income of each resident of the state, which, once again, would hit the most disadvantaged people. Also the savings of the people would suffer from devaluation, including savings of the mandatory funded pension scheme. The problems of borrowers would intensify because 85% of the credits are taken in euros. Latvia is a very small and open economy. It means that the possible benefit of [greater] competitiveness would last for a very short time and be insignificant,

because the prices of imported energy sources and components would automatically increase. Even worse, by devaluing, we would lose the "light at the end of the tunnel." We would not be able to implement "the exit strategy"—to join the euro zone in 2014.[2]

Depreciation in any form would have amounted to a big risk. Why take a big risk for no tangible advantage?

Latvian Peculiarities

As a small, old, embattled nation, Latvia is rather unique. Few nations have suffered so much and yet survived. Hopefully, suffering engenders some wisdom, and nations do learn from their historical experiences.

Latvia learned many things when it regained its independence from the Soviet Union in August 1991. Like Estonia and Lithuania, Latvia became a nation of rational heroes, people who found through their personal fate that it made sense to be heroic and stand up for their implausible dream. Latvians had gone through fire and water for their nation's independence, and they were prepared to do so again, fearing the financial crisis could undermine their sovereignty.

In the post-Soviet chaos, Latvians had learned that the best way to build a market economy and stabilize national finances was to do so swiftly and radically. A temporary decline in GDP was not very relevant for future welfare. It was far more important to get the economic system right. Therefore, in the recent crisis, Latvia benefited from an unusually good popular understanding of economics. As the *Financial Times* put it: "The vicious 1990s post-Soviet slump made Latvians hardily resourceful."[3]

Since all Latvians had faced the same dilemmas and drawn approximately the same lessons, the country was characterized by an uncommon, broad political consensus. Almost all its many parties could be described as free-market and center-right. The two main political rivals, Ivars Godmanis and I, had very similar thoughts about economic policy. The differences lay in vested interests.

Far too often, people learn only from their own experience, but Latvians benefited from also knowing the situation of their similar neighbors, especially Estonia, the most radical reformer.[4] The three Baltic countries studied each other's experiences, and Latvia's standard conclusion was to proceed with its reforms. Latvia also learned from the Swedish and Finnish banking and devaluation crises in the early 1990s that banking collapses and devaluation should be avoided if possible.

The dominant cofinancing by the European Commission and the Nordic countries reduced the traditional role of the IMF, which offered Latvian officials unusually open negotiations. As a virtuous member of the European Union, the North Atlantic Treaty Organization (NATO), and the Nordic-Baltic community, Latvia had many friends. Therefore, a huge amount of funding was available at an early stage. This was not unique but unusual.

Unlike most other countries with a fixed exchange rate, Latvia had an obvious and desired exit: adoption of the euro. This mattered to both Latvia's EU partners and the Latvian population, who favored deeper integration into the European community.

All of Eastern Europe had enjoyed a near decade of high economic growth from 2000 to 2007, but none experienced higher growth than Latvia. Many Latvians thought that they had just been too lucky and that a severe setback was inevitable. In this, they were similar to the South Koreans, who took their hardship in 1997–98 with the same surprising equanimity. After all, the average growth of Latvia even including the crisis was 42 percent for the decade 2000–10, which equaled the average growth for the new eastern EU members.[5]

Lessons from Latvia for the World

We contend that important lessons can be drawn from the resolution of Latvia's financial crisis for other countries in crisis. Walter Bagehot, founder of the *Economist* magazine, reportedly said: "The greatest pleasure in life is doing what people say you cannot do." We found time and again that in Latvia's crisis what people said could not be done was done, and it obviously was the best solution. We would like to emphasize nine lessons on the economics of financial crisis and its political economy from Latvia that are relevant for other countries.

First, devaluation was never necessary or inevitable and hardly useful because it would not have solved Latvia's problems. Latvia suffered from financial overheating, the cure of which was stopping excessive short-term capital inflows, and this did not require devaluation. The financial crisis erupted because of a too sudden stop of international liquidity, requiring mobilization of more liquidity, which was not related to devaluation. The country's competitiveness needed to improve, which was better done by reducing excessive public expenditures and salaries, and the steady exchange rate parity forced Latvia to undertake long-overdue structural reforms. The alleged risk of a vicious deflationary cycle was never real, because for a small and open economy such as Latvia, prices are largely determined by the surrounding markets. As the pass-through of inflation would have been great, devaluation would not have been effective in restoring competitiveness.

Depreciation is an overadvertised cure in current macroeconomic discourse. A series of recent IMF papers show the new openness—or confusion. One empirical study argues that intermediate exchange rate regimes have generated the best growth performance.[6] Another paper shows that exchange rate flexibility helped buffer the impact of the crisis.[7] During the boom years, the currency board countries in Eastern Europe had better fiscal balance and higher growth than the countries with floating exchange rates, and the Baltic cases show that internal devaluation is a viable option.[8] The pragmatic wisdom from the early 1990s has been restored: There is no universally preferred exchange rate policy. The best choice depends on the concrete circumstances of the country in question.[9]

Second, the value of euro accession as a goal disciplining policy was considerable and instructive to other countries in similar situations. The Latvian people were motivated by their desire for full European integration with early adoption of the euro. This desire led them to focus on two nominal anchors: a fixed exchange rate and a budget deficit below 3 percent of GDP, so that Latvia could accede to the EMU as early as possible. These two anchors brought stability and clarity to the Latvian economic policy.

Third, Latvia's experience of fiscal adjustment has convinced us of the universal advantages of carrying out as much of the belt-tightening as possible early on. Hardship is best concentrated in a short period, when people are ready for sacrifice, what Leszek Balcerowicz calls a period of "extraordinary politics."[10] Latvia succeeded because it concentrated the fiscal adjustments in the first eight months of crisis combat. The latest fourth round of belt-tightening has been limited but politically more cumbersome.

Fourth, the Latvian experience with more than three-quarters of the initial fiscal adjustment from public expenditure cuts shows that they are economically and politically preferable to tax hikes.[11] Most popular budget adjustments were the cuts of salaries and benefits of senior civil servants and state enterprise managers as well as the reduction in public service positions, while the most unpopular measure was the value-added tax (VAT) hike, and popular resistance was fierce against raising income and profit taxes. Latvians have remained strongly committed to their flat income taxes.

Fifth, the large and frontloaded international rescue effort was appropriate and has been successful. An even greater frontloading would have been advantageous, however, as most of the output contraction was caused by a sharp rise in savings, deriving from the dearth of liquidity. Both financing and reforms need to be frontloaded. Today, after the huge rescue packages for Greece, Ireland, and the euro area as a whole, it is difficult to understand that the size of the Latvian package could be controversial. Much larger emergency credits in relation to GDP were needed because of greater globalization, and the scarcity of international liquidity primarily caused the Latvian sudden stop. This crisis resolution helped break prejudices against large financial support packages with fast, early disbursements, which went to budget financing as well, since the budget deficit was primarily caused by a temporary drop in state revenues connected with the drastic output fall.

Sixth, a strange myth has evolved that affluent democracies are politically unable to undertake large cuts in public expenditures. Latvia, as well as its Baltic neighbors, showed that these vibrant democracies were perfectly capable of reducing their public expenditures by about one-tenth of GDP in one year. Social calm prevailed. Most of Latvia's fiscal adjustment—15 percent of GDP— was concentrated in the first eight months of 2009. Since these large cuts had to be selective, they facilitated structural reforms, not only reducing the capacity but also often improving the quality of public services. The Latvian case shows that macroeconomic crisis accelerated reform.[12]

Seventh, the benefits of stable government have been greatly exaggerated.[13] It is more important that a government be adequate than stable, and a precrisis government is rarely a suitable anticrisis government. Latvia benefited from being able to switch government quickly during the crisis. That was possible because of unstable coalition governments, which are inherent in a parliamentary system with proportional elections. Thus parliamentary systems with many parties, leading to coalition governments and frequent government changes, may be beneficial for the resolution of macroeconomic crises. This observation runs counter to the current literature on political economy,[14] which seems focused on ordinary policymaking that greatly differs from crisis resolution.

Eighth, the bottom line is that populism is not very popular in a serious crisis because the population understands the severity of the crisis and wants a government that can handle the crisis as forcefully as is necessary. Therefore, the Latvian anticrisis government was able to win the parliamentary elections on October 2, 2010. The government benefited from having carefully considered the social aspects of the crisis and having concluded a social partnership agreement on the main austerity policies. The big losers in the 2010 elections were oligarchs who tried to exploit populism.

Finally, the international macroeconomic discussion was not only not useful but even harmful. It indicates an intellectual and moral crisis, well illustrated in Charles Ferguson's Oscar-winning documentary film *Inside Job*. Whenever a crisis erupted anywhere, a choir of famous international economists claimed that it was "exactly" like some other recent crisis—the worse the crisis, the more popular the parallel. When the Icelandic economy blew up in early October 2008, a herd of economists claimed that the same would happen to Latvia, although Iceland had a floating exchange rate, a high interest rate, and an overblown domestic banking system. Soon, prominent economists led by *New York Times* columnist Paul Krugman claimed that "Latvia is the new Argentina." A fundamental problem is their reliance on a brief list of "stylized facts," never bothering to find out the facts on the ground.

Foreign-owned banks have been a major bone of contention in Latvia and other crisis countries in Eastern Europe. Foreign investors preferred to buy large banks with significant market power in Eastern Europe, which were on average less profitable but better capitalized than banks that remained domestically owned.[15] With access to cheaper funding at home than local banks, they became more profitable than domestic banks over time,[16] which made them committed to stay. The Swedish banks in Latvia have rightly been blamed for having lent too much in the good times, but they were also the first to sense the impending crisis and reduced their loan expansion in Latvia in mid-2007. In the midst of the crisis, credit shrank considerably throughout the world, as only a few central banks could expand liquidity. The demise of Parex Bank illustrated the danger of a large domestic bank relying on foreign, short-term wholesale finance. The four big foreign banks steeled themselves for the crisis and bore their losses themselves. Today, after the crisis, fully integrated international banks appear advantageous, but effective pan-European bank regulation is needed.[17]

The financial crisis in Latvia has been remarkable for everything that did not happen. There was no significant reaction against globalization, capitalism, the European Union, or the euro. No major strikes or social unrest erupted, while the population rose against populism and unjustified state privileges. Politically and financially, crony businessmen were the biggest losers, whereas the political winners were the moderate but decisive center-right forces. The sensible Latvian public wanted decisive action from their leaders to resolve their problems.

This political economy was reminiscent of the early postcommunist transition, when radical reform and democracy went hand in hand. The ideological wind was clearly liberal and free market but also socially responsible, favoring a somewhat purer market economy and a moderate retrenchment of the social welfare state. Latvians did not object to the welfare state as such, but they wanted social welfare to be trimmed, to become more efficient, and to work for those in need rather than being diverted to the wealthy.

In the first half of 2009, Latvia was often in the news as the country worst affected by the global financial crisis, and speculation reigned that it could be financially hazardous for the whole north European region. By late summer of 2009, the Latvian crisis had abated, and as of spring 2010, Greece, Portugal, Ireland, and Spain were the countries suffering the worst of the crisis.

Today, Latvia stands out as an example of how crises should be resolved: early, fast, and surgically, mobilizing popular understanding and support. This small nation can hopefully offer Greece and other crisis countries in the euro area lessons of radical internal devaluation, because for the EMU members devaluation is not an option.

Eyes on the Prize: Euro Adoption and European Convergence

The main goal of Latvia's economic policy is of course the long-term economic welfare of the Latvian nation, which suffered a serious setback during the crisis. GDP per capita measured in purchasing power parity may recover to 2007 levels only in 2014 (figure 7.3). Only in 2010 did GDP levels return to levels at the beginning of 2005. Three years of boom (2005–07) with a total growth of 33 percent were erased by three years of bust (2008–10), with a decline of 25 percent.

The cost of the economic overheating has been great, and it must not be repeated. Latvia should aim for high but sustainable economic growth, based on improved human capital, increased efficiency, and growing capital investment. But these are not enough. Latvia must also secure macroeconomic stability. Therefore the nation is focused on adopting the euro at the earliest opportunity, which is 2014.

A small open economy that pursues its transactions predominantly in one currency, the euro, needs to have a fixed parity to that exchange rate so that it does not become subject to the vagaries of exchange rate vacillations. Latvia should minimize the currency risks that also exist in the domestic economy

Figure 7.3   Latvia's economic convergence with the European Union, 1992–2012e

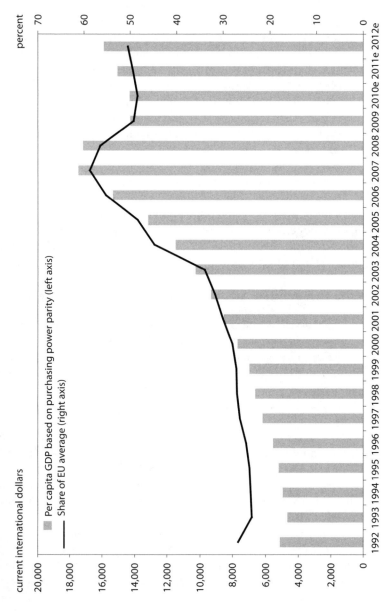

current international dollars

percent

■ Per capita GDP based on purchasing power parity (left axis)
— Share of EU average (right axis)

1992 1993 1994 1995 1996 1997 1998 1999 2000 2001 2002 2003 2004 2005 2006 2007 2008 2009 2010e 2011e 2012e

e = estimate

Source: IMF, *World Economic Outlook* database, October 2010 (accessed on November 30, 2010).

because of the far-reaching euroization of the credit market. There is no real-istic possibility of minimizing the usage of the euro within a free market such as Latvia, and so the only way of eliminating this currency risk is to adopt the euro. As we've already mentioned, the main cause of the great Latvian output decline was the sudden stop in international liquidity, which showed how vital liquidity is for Latvia. Adopting the euro would also give Latvia access to the only plau-sible large source of liquidity, the European Central Bank (ECB), which helped the euro area states with ample credit during the height of the crisis.

Two countries in the euro area, Ireland and Spain, suffered from over-heating similar to that in Latvia. They also had overblown banking sectors financed by foreign credit, with too large real estate investments. But it is unre-alistic for a very small and open European economy to regulate its banking system much more strictly than its neighbors, because banking can easily migrate abroad. Hopefully, the four new EU bodies for financial supervision among the EU nations will be able to contain asset bubbles, which were previ-ously ignored because nobody had direct responsibility. These four bodies—the European Systemic Risk Board (ESRB), European Banking Authority (EBA), European Insurance and Occupational Pensions Authority (EIOPA), and European Securities and Markets Authority (ESMA)—all began working on January 1, 2011. The ESRB, which is responsible for establishing a common list of indicators to assess the risks posed by certain financial institutions oper-ating in the European Union, would react to excessive private foreign debt and currency mismatches.[18]

The gross disregard of the fiscal Maastricht criteria or the Stability and Growth Pact by most euro area countries is not likely to be repeated. The cost of fiscal laxity is probably so evident that most nations will discipline themselves, and if not the other EMU members are likely to impose their will. This crisis has changed the economic policy mindset for a long time. Moreover, when countries with a strong record of fiscal discipline, such as Estonia and Latvia, enter the board of the ECB, monetary discipline will be further reassured.

The key question is whether Latvia—a country that has been most affected by the crisis—will in the foreseeable future become a country with a successful and modern economy, educated society, and highly qualified labor force and where best performing companies of the world are willing to invest. Latvia faces a historical choice: whether to regress to the path of stagnation and back-wardness or to identify itself as a strong nation, one of Europe's success stories, and unite in a common effort to pursue this objective.

Notes

1. International Monetary Fund, Republic of Latvia, "Third Review under the Stand-By Arrange-ment and Financing Assurances Review," July 6, 2010, 25, www.imf.org.

2. Cabinet of Ministers of the Republic of Latvia, "Address by Prime Minister Valdis Dombrovskis to the Saeima Members," State Chancellery, November 5, 2009, www.mk.gov.lv (accessed on De-cember 15, 2010).

3. "The Lex Column: Greece/Latvia," *Financial Times*, May 7, 2010.

4. Mart Laar, *The Little Country That Could* (London: Centre for Research into Post-Communist Economies, 2002).

5. Anders Åslund, *The Last Shall Be the First: The East European Financial Crisis, 2008–10* (Washington: Peterson Institute for International Economics, 2010, 49). Based on IMF forecast that has been adjusted to the actual GDP growth for 2010.

6. Atish R. Ghosh, Jonathan D. Ostry, and Charamlambos Tsangarides, "Exchange Rate Regimes and the Stability of the International Monetary System," IMF Occasional Paper no. 270 (Washington: International Monetary Fund, 2010).

7. Pelin Berkmen, Gaston Gelos, Robert Rennhack, and James Walsh, "The Global Financial Crisis: Explaining Cross-Country Differences in the Output Impact," IMF Working Paper 09/280 (Washington: International Monetary Fund, 2009).

8. Åslund, *The Last Shall Be the First*, 111–12.

9. Stanley Fischer, "Exchange Rates: Is the Bipolar View Correct," in *IMF Essays from a Time of Crisis: The International Financial System, Stabilization, and Development*, Stanley Fischer (Cambridge, MA: MIT Press, 2005, 227–54).

10. Leszek Balcerowicz, "Understanding Postcommunist Transitions," *Journal of Democracy* 5, no. 4 (1994): 75–89.

11. This argument has been made well by Vito Tanzi and Ludger Schuknecht, *Public Spending in the 20th Century* (Cambridge: Cambridge University Press, 2000).

12. Allen Drazen and Vittorio Grilli, "The Benefit of Crises for Economic Reforms," *American Economic Review* 83, no. 3 (1993): 598–607.

13. Some political scientists even see political stability as a goal in itself: Jon Elster, Claus Offe, and Ulrich K. Preuss, *Institutional Design in Post Communist Societies* (Cambridge: Cambridge University Press, 1998, 292–93).

14. Torsten Persson and Guido Tabellini have spearheaded it in *Political Economics: Explaining Economic Policy* (Cambridge, MA: MIT Press, 2000); *Economic Effects of Constitutions* (Cambridge, MA: MIT Press, 2003); and "Constitutions and Economic Policy," *Journal of Economic Perspectives* 18, no. 1 (Winter 2004): 75–98.

15. Olena Havrylchyk and Emilia Jurzyk, "Inherited or Earned? Performance of Foreign Banks in Central and Eastern Europe," IMF Working Paper 10/4 (Washington: International Monetary Fund, 2010).

16. John Bonin, Iftekhar Hasan, and Paul Wachtel, "Bank Performance, Efficiency and Ownership in Transition Countries," *Journal of Banking and Finance* 29, no. 1 (2005): 31–53; R. De Haas and I. van Lelyveld, "Foreign Banks and Credit Stability in Central and Eastern Europe: A Panel Data Analysis," *Journal of Banking and Finance* 30 (2006): 1927–52.

17. Peter Zajc, "A Comparative Study of Bank Efficiency in Central and Eastern Europe: The Role of Foreign Ownership," *International Finance Review* 6 (2006): 117–56; Rainer Haselmann, "Strategies of Foreign Banks in Transition Economies," *Emerging Markets Review* 7, no. 4 (December 2006): 283–99.

18. The European Banking Authority is based in London, the European Insurance and Occupational Pensions Authority and the European Systemic Risk Board in Frankfurt, and the European Securities and Markets Authority in Paris. The EBA would react if something like the Swedish bank expansion to Latvia of 2005–06 recurred.

Leading Latvian Officials

Dombrovskis, Valdis. Born in 1971. Prime minister since 2009; minister of finance, 2002–04; member of the European Parliament; leader of New Era.

Godmanis, Ivars. Born in 1951. Member of the European Parliament; Latvia's prime minister, 1990–93 and 2007–09; leader of Latvia's First Party/Latvia's Way.

Kalvītis, Aigars. Born in 1966. Chairman of the board of Latvijas Balzams corporation; leader of People's Party; prime minister, 2004–07.

Lembergs, Aivars. Born in 1953. Mayor of Ventspils since 1988; leading businessman; informal leader of the Union of Greens and Farmers.

Repše, Einars. Born in 1961. Chairman of the Bank of Latvia, 1991–2001; prime minister, 2002–04; minister of finance, 2009–10; and founder of New Era.

Rimšēvičs, Ilmārs. Born in 1966. Governor of the Bank of Latvia since December 2001; no party affiliation.

Šķēle, Andris. Born in 1958. Leading businessman; prime minister 1995–97 and 1999–2000; leader of People's Party.

Slakteris, Atis. Born in 1956. Leader of People's Party; minister of defense, 2004–08; minister of finance, 2008–09.

Šlesers, Ainārs. Born in 1970. Leading businessman; leader of Latvia's First Party/Latvia's Way; minister of transportation, 2004–09; minister of economy, 1998–99.

Urbanovičs, Jānis. Born in 1959. Member of parliament; leader of Harmony Center.

Ušakovs, Nils. Born in 1976. Mayor of Riga since 2009; leader of Harmony Center.

Zatlers, Valdis. Born in 1956. President since July 2007; surgeon; no party affiliation.

Chronology of Events

Date	Event
November 18, 1918	Latvian National Council proclaims Latvia an independent and sovereign state.
1919–20	Liberation war.
August 11, 1920	Latvia signs peace treaty with Soviet Russia, in which Soviet Russia recognizes Latvian independence and sovereignty.
August 23, 1939	The Soviet Union and Nazi Germany conclude the Molotov-Ribbentrop Non-Aggression Pact, awarding the three Baltic states to the Soviet Union.
June 1940	Soviet troops invade Latvia, incorporating it into the Soviet Union along with Estonia and Lithuania.
June 1941	Nazi German forces invade.
1944	The Red Army returns and occupies Latvia. Latvia is sovietized.
March 1990	The Latvian Popular Front wins two-thirds majority in the first reasonably free elections since Soviet occupation during World War II.

(Chronology continues next page)

Date	Event
May 1990	The Latvian parliament declares "de jure" independence of the Republic of Latvia. Ivars Godmanis of the Latvian Popular Front becomes prime minister.
August 21, 1991	At the end of the abortive hard-line coup in Moscow, the Latvian parliament passes the constitutional law declaring Latvia an independent, democratic republic according to the 1922 constitution.
September 6, 1991	The Soviet Union recognizes Latvia's independence.
September 17, 1991	Latvia becomes a member of the United Nations.
May 19, 1992	Latvia joins the International Monetary Fund (IMF) and the World Bank.
July 1992	Latvia breaks out of the ruble zone and establishes its own currency, the lat.
September 1992	Latvia concludes its first IMF stand-by program.
June 1993	The first truly free elections to the Latvian 100-seat parliament take place.
August 31, 1994	The last Russian troops leave Latvian territory.
1995	Banking crisis hits Latvia.
October 13, 1995	Latvia applies for EU membership.
August 17, 1998	Russia devalues and defaults on its domestic bonds.
February 10, 1999	Latvia becomes a member of the World Trade Organization (WTO).
October 13, 1999	European Commission recommends that member states open membership negotiations with Latvia.
March 29, 2004	Latvia becomes a member of the North Atlantic Treaty Organization (NATO).
May 1, 2004	Latvia becomes a member of the European Union.
October 2006	Parliamentary elections take place in Latvia. Parties in coalition government led by Aigars Kalvītis win parliamentary majority.
March 2007	Latvia signs border demarcation treaty with Russia.

Date	Event
December 2007	Prime Minister Kalvītis resigns over his attempts to sack the country's anticorruption chief. The same coalition returns to power but with Ivars Godmanis as new prime minister.
2008	
September 15	Lehman Brothers goes bankrupt. Global liquidity freezes.
October 28	The IMF announces staff-level agreement with Hungary on €12.5 billion loan ($15.7 billion).
November 6	The IMF Executive Board approves $15.7 billion, 17-month Stand-By Arrangement for Hungary, making $6.3 billion immediately available.
November 14	The Latvian parliament adopts budget for 2009.
November 19	Hungary signs a memorandum of understanding with ECOFIN Council for assistance of up to €6.5 billion.
December 19	The IMF announces staff-level agreement with Latvia on a €1.7 billion Stand-By Arrangement as part of a coordinated international financial support package of €7.5 billion.
December 23	IMF Executive Board approves $2.35 billion, 27-month Stand-By Arrangement for Latvia and disburses a first installment of €586 million ($860 million).
2009	
January 13	Hundreds of demonstrators clash with police in Riga.
January 20	The ECOFIN Council approves medium-term financial assistance for Latvia totaling €3.1 billion under the balance of payments facility for non–euro area member states.
January 26	Memorandum of understanding signed in Riga for the European Union to provide up to €3.1 billion financial assistance to Latvia.
February 20	Prime Minister Godmanis resigns. Ruling coalition collapses amid widespread popular discontent.
February 25	The European Commission disburses the first installment to Latvia of €1 billion.

(Chronology continues next page)

Date	Event
March 12	Valdis Dombrovskis is sworn in as prime minister of a new five-party coalition government.
March 25	IMF announces staff-level agreement with Romania on €12.95 billion loan as part of coordinated financial support.
May 4	IMF Executive Board approves $17.1 billion, 24-month Stand-By Arrangement for Romania.
June 6	Local elections and European parliamentary elections in Latvia.
June	The Latvian government, trade unions, and employers agree on deep public spending cuts in a supplementary budget.
July 2	The European Commission decides to disburse the second installment of €1.2 billion on July 27.
July 27	The IMF reaches staff-level agreement with the Latvian authorities on first review under Stand-By Arrangement.
August 27	The IMF completes first review under Stand-By Arrangement with Latvia and approves €195 million ($279 million), bringing total disbursements to €781 million ($1.14 billion).
December 1	The parliament adopts budget for 2010.
2010	
February 17	The IMF completes second review under Stand-By Arrangement with Latvia and approves €200 million ($275 million) disbursement, bringing total disbursements to €1 billion ($1.37 billion).
February 26	A new supplementary memorandum of understanding is concluded with the European Union.
March 11	The European Commission disburses its third installment to Latvia of €500 million.
March	People's Party, the largest coalition party, leaves government following repeated disagreements over austerity measures, depriving the government of its majority.
May 2	EU summit on the Greek financial crisis.
May 9–10	EU summit on the eurozone financial crisis.
July 13, 2011	EU finance ministers permit Estonia to adopt the euro on January 1, 2011.

Date	Event
July 21	The IMF completes third review under Stand-By Arrangement with Latvia and approves €106 million ($136 million) disbursement, bringing total disbursements to €1.15 billion ($1.48 billion).
October 2	Parliamentary elections take place in Latvia. The incumbent Dombrovskis government wins.
November 3	Dombrovskis forms a majority two-bloc government with the Union of Farmers and Greens.
December 20	The parliament adopts budget for 2011.

Sources: Icon Group International, *Latvia: Webster's Timeline History, 1054–2007* (ICON Group International, Inc., 2010); Latvian Institute, "History of Latvia: A Timeline," www.li.lv (accessed on November 21, 2010); BBC News, Latvian Timeline, November 4, 2010, http://news.bbc.co.uk; International Monetary Fund, www.imf.org; Gateway to the European Union, http://europa.eu/index_en.htm.

Index

international repercussions, of devaluation, 53, 115–16
international reserves, 79, 80*f*, 84, 104
investment-saving ratio, 20–21, 22*f*, 25, 26*f*, 102, 103*t*
Ireland, 95, 119, 121, 123

Kalvītis, Aigars, 30, 31, 33, 127
Kampars, Artis, 68, 97
Kargins, Valerijs, 35, 39
Keynesian stimulus, 56
KNAB. *See* Corruption Prevention and Combating Bureau
Kosovo, 54
Krasovickis, Viktors, 35, 39
Krugman, Paul, 4, 55, 60, 120

labor market. *See also* unemployment
during credit boom, 22–23, 23*f*
Latvian Communist Party, 6, 13
Latvian Confederation of Employers, 40
Latvian financial crisis
chronology of events, 129–33
credit boom preceding (*See* credit boom)
end of (*See* crisis resolution)
international financing for (*See* international assistance package)
leading officials, 127–28 (*See also specific official*)
lessons from, 3–4, 88, 113–25
as model, 1–2, 96
peculiarities, 117–18
political economy of (*See* political economy)
Latvian-Soviet Peace Treaty, 5
"Latvia's Economic Stabilization and Growth Revival Program," 41–42
Latvia's First Party/Latvia's Way, 30–31, 34
electoral results, 79, 99*t*
in For a Good Latvia bloc, 97
as opposition, 67
Latvia's National Independence movement, 67
leftwing rhetoric, 57
Lehman Brothers bankruptcy, 33, 35
Lembergs, Aivars, 30, 79, 127
lessons
exchange rate devaluation, 3, 113–19
financial crisis, 3–4, 88, 113–25
international aspects, 118–21
post-Soviet transition, 117
Lithuania
banking market, 20
currency board, 51
effects of devaluation on, 53, 116
EU accession, 18

euro adoption, 96
internal devaluation, 2, 56–57
Soviet occupation of, 5–7
tax system, 89
local elections, 79

Maastricht criteria, 18, 77*b*
ability to meet, 27, 53, 58, 62
budget deficit, 18, 30, 34, 53, 68, 89
Estonia, 96
euro area disregard for, 123
exchange rate, 18, 43
inflation, 18, 21, 53
interest rate, 18
public debt, 18, 102
manufacturing sector, 103–104
market economy transition, 7–11
Master Plan on Optimization of the Hospital Network, 73
Merkel, Angela, 78
military expenditures, 37
Molotov-Ribbentrop Non-Aggression Pact, 5–6
monetary policy
Bank of Latvia, 8, 39, 102, 113–14
European Central Bank, 20, 29
post-Soviet transition, 8–9
US Federal Reserve, 20, 29
Montenegro, 54
Mortgage and Land Bank (MLB), 104

NATO (North Atlantic Treaty Organization), 7, 17, 18, 37, 82
New Era, 31
budget policy, 37
electoral results, 36, 82, 98, 99*t*
government formed by, 65, 67–69
on stabilization program, 40–41
in Unity bloc, 97
Nordea, 19–20
Nordic countries. *See also specific country*
assistance from, 46, 46*t*, 85 (*See also* international assistance package)
Norway, assistance from, 46, 46*t*

oligarchs. *See also specific party or leader*
in coalition government, 69
consolidation of, 97
during credit boom, 30
decline of, 82, 98, 120
post-Soviet, 10
reform opposed by, 13–14

Other Publications from the
Peterson Institute for
International Economics

WORKING PAPERS

92 China's Strategy to Secure Natural Resources: Risks, Dangers, and Opportunities   Theodore H. Moran
June 2010   ISBN 978-088132-512-6
93 The Implications of China-Taiwan Economic Liberalization
Daniel H. Rosen and Zhi Wang
January 2011   ISBN 978-0-88132-501-0

BOOKS

IMF Conditionality*   John Williamson, ed.
1983   ISBN 0-88132-006-4
Trade Policy in the 1980s*   William R. Cline, ed.
1983   ISBN 0-88132-031-5
Subsidies in International Trade*
Gary Clyde Hufbauer and Joanna Shelton Erb
1984   ISBN 0-88132-004-8
International Debt: Systemic Risk and Policy Response*   William R. Cline
1984   ISBN 0-88132-015-3
Trade Protection in the United States: 31 Case Studies*   Gary Clyde Hufbauer,
Diane E. Berliner, and Kimberly Ann Elliott
1986   ISBN 0-88132-040-4
Toward Renewed Economic Growth in Latin America*   Bela Balassa, Gerardo M. Bueno, Pedro Pablo Kuczynski, and Mario Henrique Simonsen
1986   ISBN 0-88132-045-5
Capital Flight and Third World Debt*
Donald R. Lessard and John Williamson, eds.
1987   ISBN 0-88132-053-6
The Canada-United States Free Trade Agreement: The Global Impact*
Jeffrey J. Schott and Murray G. Smith, eds.
1988   ISBN 0-88132-073-0
World Agricultural Trade: Building a Consensus*   William M. Miner and Dale E. Hathaway, eds.
1988   ISBN 0-88132-071-3
Japan in the World Economy*   Bela Balassa and Marcus Noland
1988   ISBN 0-88132-041-2
America in the World Economy: A Strategy for the 1990s*   C. Fred Bergsten
1988   ISBN 0-88132-089-7
Managing the Dollar: From the Plaza to the Louvre*   Yoichi Funabashi
1988, 2d ed. 1989   ISBN 0-88132-097-8
United States External Adjustment and the World Economy*   William R. Cline
May 1989   ISBN 0-88132-048-X
Free Trade Areas and U.S. Trade Policy*
Jeffrey J. Schott, ed.
May 1989   ISBN 0-88132-094-3
Dollar Politics: Exchange Rate Policymaking in the United States*   I. M. Destler and C. Randall Henning
September 1989   ISBN 0-88132-079-X
Latin American Adjustment: How Much Has Happened?*   John Williamson, ed.
April 1990   ISBN 0-88132-125-7

The Future of World Trade in Textiles and Apparel*   William R. Cline
1987, 2d ed. June 1999   ISBN 0-88132-110-9
Completing the Uruguay Round: A Results-Oriented Approach to the GATT Trade Negotiations*   Jeffrey J. Schott, ed.
September 1990   ISBN 0-88132-130-3
Economic Sanctions Reconsidered (2 volumes)
Economic Sanctions Reconsidered: Supplemental Case Histories
Gary Clyde Hufbauer, Jeffrey J. Schott, and Kimberly Ann Elliott
1985, 2d ed. Dec. 1990   ISBN cloth 0-88132-115-X
          ISBN paper 0-88132-105-2
Economic Sanctions Reconsidered: History and Current Policy   Gary Clyde Hufbauer, Jeffrey J. Schott, and Kimberly Ann Elliott
December 1990   ISBN cloth 0-88132-140-0
          ISBN paper 0-88132-136-2
Pacific Basin Developing Countries: Prospects for the Future*   Marcus Noland
January 1991   ISBN cloth 0-88132-141-9
          ISBN paper 0-88132-081-1
Currency Convertibility in Eastern Europe*
John Williamson, ed.
October 1991   ISBN 0-88132-128-1
International Adjustment and Financing: The Lessons of 1985-1991*   C. Fred Bergsten, ed.
January 1992   ISBN 0-88132-112-5
North American Free Trade: Issues and Recommendations*   Gary Clyde Hufbauer and Jeffrey J. Schott
April 1992   ISBN 0-88132-120-6
Narrowing the U.S. Current Account Deficit*
Alan J. Lenz
June 1992   ISBN 0-88132-103-6
The Economics of Global Warming
William R. Cline
June 1992   ISBN 0-88132-132-X
US Taxation of International Income: Blueprint for Reform   Gary Clyde Hufbauer, assisted by Joanna M. van Rooij
October 1992   ISBN 0-88132-134-6
Who's Bashing Whom? Trade Conflict in High-Technology Industries   Laura D'Andrea Tyson
November 1992   ISBN 0-88132-106-0
Korea in the World Economy*   Il SaKong
January 1993   ISBN 0-88132-183-4
Pacific Dynamism and the International Economic System*   C. Fred Bergsten and Marcus Noland, eds.
May 1993   ISBN 0-88132-196-6
Economic Consequences of Soviet Disintegration*   John Williamson, ed.
May 1993   ISBN 0-88132-190-7
Reconcilable Differences? United States-Japan Economic Conflict*   C. Fred Bergsten and Marcus Noland
June 1993   ISBN 0-88132-129-X
Does Foreign Exchange Intervention Work?
Kathryn M. Dominguez and Jeffrey A. Frankel
September 1993   ISBN 0-88132-104-4

Trade and Income Distribution
William R. Cline
November 1997   ISBN 0-88132-216-4
Global Competition Policy
Edward M. Graham and J. David Richardson
December 1997   ISBN 0-88132-166-4
**Unfinished Business: Telecommunications
after the Uruguay Round**
Gary Clyde Hufbauer and Erika Wada
December 1997   ISBN 0-88132-257-1
Financial Services Liberalization in the WTO
Wendy Dobson and Pierre Jacquet
June 1998   ISBN 0-88132-254-7
Restoring Japan's Economic Growth
Adam S. Posen
September 1998   ISBN 0-88132-262-8
Measuring the Costs of Protection in China
Zhang Shuguang, Zhang Yansheng, and Wan
Zhongxin
November 1998   ISBN 0-88132-247-4
**Foreign Direct Investment and Development:
The New Policy Agenda for Developing
Countries and Economies in Transition**
Theodore H. Moran
December 1998   ISBN 0-88132-258-X
**Behind the Open Door: Foreign Enterprises
in the Chinese Marketplace**   Daniel H. Rosen
January 1999   ISBN 0-88132-263-6
**Toward A New International Financial
Architecture: A Practical Post-Asia Agenda**
Barry Eichengreen
February 1999   ISBN 0-88132-270-9
Is the U.S. Trade Deficit Sustainable?
Catherine L. Mann
September 1999   ISBN 0-88132-265-2
**Safeguarding Prosperity in a Global Financial
System: The Future International Financial
Architecture, Independent Task Force Report
Sponsored by the Council on Foreign Relations**
Morris Goldstein, Project Director
October 1999   ISBN 0-88132-287-3
**Avoiding the Apocalypse: The Future of the
Two Koreas**   Marcus Noland
June 2000   ISBN 0-88132-278-4
**Assessing Financial Vulnerability: An Early
Warning System for Emerging Markets**
Morris Goldstein, Graciela Kaminsky, and
Carmen Reinhart
June 2000   ISBN 0-88132-237-7
Global Electronic Commerce: A Policy Primer
Catherine L. Mann, Sue E. Eckert, and Sarah
Cleeland Knight
July 2000   ISBN 0-88132-274-1
The WTO after Seattle   Jeffrey J. Schott, ed.
July 2000   ISBN 0-88132-290-3
**Intellectual Property Rights in the Global
Economy**   Keith E. Maskus
August 2000   ISBN 0-88132-282-2
**The Political Economy of the Asian Financial
Crisis**   Stephan Haggard
August 2000   ISBN 0-88132-283-0
**Transforming Foreign Aid: United States
Assistance in the 21st Century**   Carol Lancaster
August 2000   ISBN 0-88132-291-1

**Fighting the Wrong Enemy: Antiglobal
Activists and Multinational Enterprises**
Edward M. Graham
September 2000   ISBN 0-88132-272-5
**Globalization and the Perceptions of American
Workers**   Kenneth Scheve and
Matthew J. Slaughter
March 2001   ISBN 0-88132-295-4
World Capital Markets: Challenge to the G-10
Wendy Dobson and Gary Clyde Hufbauer,
assisted by Hyun Koo Cho
May 2001   ISBN 0-88132-301-2
Prospects for Free Trade in the Americas
Jeffrey J. Schott
August 2001   ISBN 0-88132-275-X
**Toward a North American Community:
Lessons from the Old World for the New**
Robert A. Pastor
August 2001   ISBN 0-88132-328-4
**Measuring the Costs of Protection in Europe:
European Commercial Policy in the 2000s**
Patrick A. Messerlin
September 2001   ISBN 0-88132-273-3
Job Loss from Imports: Measuring the Costs
Lori G. Kletzer
September 2001   ISBN 0-88132-296-2
**No More Bashing: Building a New Japan–
United States Economic Relationship**
C. Fred Bergsten, Takatoshi Ito, and Marcus
Noland
October 2001   ISBN 0-88132-286-5
Why Global Commitment Really Matters!
Howard Lewis III and J. David Richardson
October 2001   ISBN 0-88132-298-9
Leadership Selection in the Major Multilaterals
Miles Kahler
November 2001   ISBN 0-88132-335-7
**The International Financial Architecture:
What's New? What's Missing?**   Peter B. Kenen
November 2001   ISBN 0-88132-297-0
**Delivering on Debt Relief: From IMF Gold to a
New Aid Architecture**   John Williamson and
Nancy Birdsall, with Brian Deese
April 2002   ISBN 0-88132-331-4
**Imagine There's No Country: Poverty,
Inequality, and Growth in the Era of
Globalization**   Surjit S. Bhalla
September 2002   ISBN 0-88132-348-9
Reforming Korea's Industrial Conglomerates
Edward M. Graham
January 2003   ISBN 0-88132-337-3
**Industrial Policy in an Era of Globalization:
Lessons from Asia**   Marcus Noland and
Howard Pack
March 2003   ISBN 0-88132-350-0
Reintegrating India with the World Economy
T. N. Srinivasan and Suresh D. Tendulkar
March 2003   ISBN 0-88132-280-6
**After the Washington Consensus: Restarting
Growth and Reform in Latin America**
Pedro-Pablo Kuczynski and John Williamson, eds.
March 2003   ISBN 0-88132-347-0

The Decline of US Labor Unions and the Role of Trade Robert E. Baldwin
June 2003 ISBN 0-88132-341-1

Can Labor Standards Improve under Globalization? Kimberly Ann Elliott and Richard B. Freeman
June 2003 ISBN 0-88132-332-2

Crimes and Punishments? Retaliation under the WTO Robert Z. Lawrence
October 2003 ISBN 0-88132-359-4

Inflation Targeting in the World Economy Edwin M. Truman
October 2003 ISBN 0-88132-345-4

Foreign Direct Investment and Tax Competition John H. Mutti
November 2003 ISBN 0-88132-352-7

Has Globalization Gone Far Enough? The Costs of Fragmented Markets
Scott C. Bradford and Robert Z. Lawrence
February 2004 ISBN 0-88132-349-7

Food Regulation and Trade: Toward a Safe and Open Global System Tim Josling, Donna Roberts, and David Orden
March 2004 ISBN 0-88132-346-2

Controlling Currency Mismatches in Emerging Markets Morris Goldstein and Philip Turner
April 2004 ISBN 0-88132-360-8

Free Trade Agreements: US Strategies and Priorities Jeffrey J. Schott, ed.
April 2004 ISBN 0-88132-361-6

Trade Policy and Global Poverty William R. Cline
June 2004 ISBN 0-88132-365-9

Bailouts or Bail-ins? Responding to Financial Crises in Emerging Economies
Nouriel Roubini and Brad Setser
August 2004 ISBN 0-88132-371-3

Transforming the European Economy
Martin Neil Baily and Jacob Funk Kirkegaard
September 2004 ISBN 0-88132-343-8

Chasing Dirty Money: The Fight Against Money Laundering Peter Reuter and Edwin M. Truman
November 2004 ISBN 0-88132-370-5

The United States and the World Economy: Foreign Economic Policy for the Next Decade
C. Fred Bergsten
January 2005 ISBN 0-88132-380-2

Does Foreign Direct Investment Promote Development? Theodore H. Moran, Edward M. Graham, and Magnus Blomström, eds.
April 2005 ISBN 0-88132-381-0

American Trade Politics, 4th ed. I. M. Destler
June 2005 ISBN 0-88132-382-9

Why Does Immigration Divide America? Public Finance and Political Opposition to Open Borders Gordon H. Hanson
August 2005 ISBN 0-88132-400-0

Reforming the US Corporate Tax
Gary Clyde Hufbauer and Paul L. E. Grieco
September 2005 ISBN 0-88132-384-5

The United States as a Debtor Nation
William R. Cline
September 2005 ISBN 0-88132-399-3

NAFTA Revisited: Achievements and Challenges Gary Clyde Hufbauer and Jeffrey J. Schott, assisted by Paul L. E. Grieco and Yee Wong
October 2005 ISBN 0-88132-334-9

US National Security and Foreign Direct Investment Edward M. Graham and David M. Marchick
May 2006 ISBN 978-0-88132-391-7

Accelerating the Globalization of America: The Role for Information Technology
Catherine L. Mann, assisted by Jacob Funk Kirkegaard
June 2006 ISBN 978-0-88132-390-0

Delivering on Doha: Farm Trade and the Poor Kimberly Ann Elliott
July 2006 ISBN 978-0-88132-392-4

Case Studies in US Trade Negotiation, Vol. 1: Making the Rules Charan Devereaux, Robert Z. Lawrence, and Michael Watkins
September 2006 ISBN 978-0-88132-362-7

Case Studies in US Trade Negotiation, Vol. 2: Resolving Disputes Charan Devereaux, Robert Z. Lawrence, and Michael Watkins
September 2006 ISBN 978-0-88132-363-2

C. Fred Bergsten and the World Economy
Michael Mussa, ed.
December 2006 ISBN 978-0-88132-397-9

Working Papers, Volume I Peterson Institute
December 2006 ISBN 978-0-88132-388-7

The Arab Economies in a Changing World
Marcus Noland and Howard Pack
April 2007 ISBN 978-0-88132-393-1

Working Papers, Volume II Peterson Institute
April 2007 ISBN 978-0-88132-404-4

Global Warming and Agriculture: Impact Estimates by Country William R. Cline
July 2007 ISBN 978-0-88132-403-7

US Taxation of Foreign Income
Gary Clyde Hufbauer and Ariel Assa
October 2007 ISBN 978-0-88132-405-1

Russia's Capitalist Revolution: Why Market Reform Succeeded and Democracy Failed
Anders Åslund
October 2007 ISBN 978-0-88132-409-9

Economic Sanctions Reconsidered, 3d ed.
Gary Clyde Hufbauer, Jeffrey J. Schott, Kimberly Ann Elliott, and Barbara Oegg
November 2007
ISBN hardcover 978-0-88132-407-5
ISBN hardcover/CD-ROM 978-0-88132-408-2

Debating China's Exchange Rate Policy
Morris Goldstein and Nicholas R. Lardy, eds.
April 2008 ISBN 978-0-88132-415-0

Leveling the Carbon Playing Field: International Competition and US Climate Policy Design Trevor Houser, Rob Bradley, Britt Childs, Jacob Werksman, and Robert Heilmayr
May 2008 ISBN 978-0-88132-420-4

**Australia, New Zealand,
and Papua New Guinea**
D. A. Information Services
648 Whitehorse Road
Mitcham, Victoria 3132, Australia
Tel: 61-3-9210-7777
Fax: 61-3-9210-7788
Email: service@dadirect.com.au
www.dadirect.com.au

India, Bangladesh, Nepal, and Sri Lanka
Viva Books Private Limited
Mr. Vinod Vasishtha
4737/23 Ansari Road
Daryaganj, New Delhi 110002
India
Tel: 91-11-4224-2200
Fax: 91-11-4224-2240
Email: viva@vivagroupindia.net
www.vivagroupindia.com

**Mexico, Central America, South America,
and Puerto Rico**
US PubRep, Inc.
311 Dean Drive
Rockville, MD 20851
Tel: 301-838-9276
Fax: 301-838-9278
Email: c.falk@ieee.org

Asia (*Brunei, Burma, Cambodia, China,
Hong Kong, Indonesia, Korea, Laos, Malaysia,
Philippines, Singapore, Taiwan, Thailand,
and Vietnam*)
East-West Export Books (EWEB)
University of Hawaii Press
2840 Kolowalu Street
Honolulu, Hawaii 96822-1888
Tel: 808-956-8830
Fax: 808-988-6052
Email: eweb@hawaii.edu

Canada
Renouf Bookstore
5369 Canotek Road, Unit 1
Ottawa, Ontario KlJ 9J3, Canada
Tel: 613-745-2665
Fax: 613-745-7660
www.renoufbooks.com

Japan
United Publishers Services Ltd.
1-32-5, Higashi-shinagawa
Shinagawa-ku, Tokyo 140-0002
Japan
Tel: 81-3-5479-7251
Fax: 81-3-5479-7307
Email: purchasing@ups.co.jp
*For trade accounts only. Individuals will find
Institute books in leading Tokyo bookstores.*

Middle East
MERIC
2 Bahgat Ali Street, El Masry Towers
Tower D, Apt. 24
Zamalek, Cairo
Egypt
Tel. 20-2-7633824
Fax: 20-2-7369355
Email: mahmoud_fouda@mericonline.com
www.mericonline.com

United Kingdom, Europe
(*including Russia and Turkey*)**, Africa,
and Israel**
The Eurospan Group
c/o Turpin Distribution
Pegasus Drive
Stratton Business Park
Biggleswade, Bedfordshire
SG18 8TQ
United Kingdom
Tel: 44 (0) 1767-604972
Fax: 44 (0) 1767-601640
Email: eurospan@turpin-distribution.com
www.eurospangroup.com/bookstore

**Visit our website at:
www.piie.com
E-mail orders to:
petersonmail@presswarehouse.com**